CAUSE AND SYMPTOMS OF NARCISSIST PERSONALITY DISORDER

Interpersonal Relations in Narcissist Disorder, From Narcissist Myth to Phenomenology

Michelle White

TABLE OF CONTENTS

SYNOPSIS

You've never met a narcissist and are presently dependent upon their personality disorder? Is it accurate to say that you are in the throes of an injurious association with a narcissist?

Individuals with Narcissistic Personality Disorder have an elitist, unrivaled mentality, need sympathy and empathy for other people, feel everything in their life is substantially more significant than any other person, and can be savage to individuals who represent a danger to their overstated vision of themselves.

The reasons for this personality disorder have no answer that is authoritative in pinpointing how the narcissistic personality disorder (NPD) shows or at what age. It is potentially the blend of specific personality qualities and outer triggers.

There is inquiry about that focuses on the proposal that misuse, hereditary qualities, and different disorders can add to how narcissistic personality disorder can create.

The turmoil has been seen as terrible to individuals who have had associations with narcissists. An individual who is well-offset has sound associations with their family, companions, and colleagues and has numerous attributes that a narcissist doesn't have represents a risk to an individual with NPD.

The narcissist's condition will trigger fanatical jealousy and sentiments of low confidence, the genuine emotions that are concealed by their better acting and will provoke them to assault that individual by downgrading them, cutting down their confidence and offending them either in broad daylight or in private; it truly doesn't make a difference to the narcissist. They need sympathy and empathy.

Individuals who are engaged with an association with an individual with NPD need to comprehend what kind of narcissist they are managing.

There are various sorts and sub-types, each with their novel qualities. There is such a lot of data that is contained right now you to find and comprehend the narcissistic personality disorder. A portion of the features are:

- A away from and clarification of narcissistic personality disorder
- The signs and manifestations of narcissistic personality disorder
- Why narcissists feel they're better than every other person and the genuine hidden reasons why they feel that way and treat others inadequately
- Different kinds of narcissistic sorts and why there is one sort that an individual should never get associated with
- Victims of narcissistic maltreatment and how barbarous and destructive a narcissistic injurious relationship can harm the unfortunate casualty's confidence and soul and the trouble of releasing this sort of relationship

- The phases of recuperation that a casualty of narcissistic maltreatment needs to experience to so as to get mended and entire once more
- ...and a whole lot more!

In the event that you are intrigued on finding out about narcissistic personality disorder and its impacts on the individuals who experience the ill effects of it just as the individuals who experience the ill effects of being in injurious associations with an individual with this kind of confusion, this book is for you.

In the wake of reading this book you will discover substantially more about the narcissistic personality disorder and comprehend its impacts on others, and how an individual might be engaged with them.

INTRODUCTION

Have you at any point had an association with a narcissist? A parent, kin, companion, or critical other? A few people get on them moderately rapidly yet some don't perceive the admonition signs and that can wind up being terrible for them.

Right now, personality Disorder: A self-improvement Recovery Emotional Guide to comprehend the reasons for narcissism and how to endure Narcissistic maltreatment in any sort of Relationship, you will adapt exactly what a narcissistic personality disorder (NPD) is, the thing that the particular indications of an individual with NPD, how this personality disorder can be hard and damaging and how an individual can get manhandled and damaged by an individual with this personality disorder.

Narcissists are at first extremely beguiling, shrewd, and even enjoyable to be with. Anyway underneath this lovely façade is somebody who needs sympathy, feels they are "entitled" to be dealt with in an unexpected way, feel that the vast majority are not their equivalents, and accept they are predominant.

The parts that follow will give you a review of the narcissistic personality condition, just as its causes, the signs and side effects, the various sorts of NPD, and how to manage an individual who has a narcissistic personality.

This book is composed to assist individuals with distinguishing an individual with NPD or on the off chance that you are as of now seeing someone, advantage from the assets furnished to help you in managing an individual who might be mentally hurtful to you and help you in managing them.

You've sufficiently experienced, and now, it's an ideal opportunity to mend. It may have taken you some time, yet you're here and you're headed to a fuller, happier life, away from the maltreatment. In this way, take a full breath, grin, and give yourself a congratulatory gesture. It unquestionably wasn't simple.

Being the casualty of a narcissist can be depleting, debilitating, and excruciating. For some, the maltreatment can traverse a long time without resolve, making it harder, and harder to get away from the circumstance with each spending day. Sadly, the more you remain with a narcissist, the more profound you fall into their snare, turning out to be increasingly more ensnared in their web as they keep on fixing their hold around your neck.

In any case, on the off chance that you're reading this now, at that point that means you've just experienced the hardest part, and that is something to be pleased with. A large number of the individuals who endure narcissistic connections guarantee that it wants to be stuck in an endless loop – the abuser controls your considerations, you're customized to satisfy them, and the poisonous quality of the relationship is covered by reprimanding you for each easily overlooked detail that turns out badly. So truly, at long last settling on the choice to simply leave is something to celebrate.

All in all, what happens now? What occurs after you've left? How would you manage these sentiments of blame, disgrace, and bitterness? What are you expected to do in the event that you feel like it's smarter to return, apologize, and become a machine gear-piece in the narcissist's framework again? Imagine a scenario in which you need them back in your life.

What happens now?

While the hardest piece of the procedure is leaving, mending in the wake of going separate ways with a narcissist can be about as troublesome. The instruments they set up might in any case be in activity, making it difficult for you to recognize the truth about the maltreatment. Despite the fact that it may be extreme and in spite of the fact that you may feel like there's no closure to the torment and blame, you'd be calmed to discover that mending is conceivable.

Furthermore, it becomes much more of a reality when you follow guides this way.

On the off chance that it's any relief, you should realize that you're not the first to have experienced narcissistic maltreatment. Innumerable others before you have seen the harmed, disloyalty, and trouble, and they've recuperated from the long periods of abuse to turn out to be better, fuller, more joyful individuals with satisfying connections and a more prominent feeling of self-esteem.

What you can be sure of is that that is something you can have, as well.

In this way, in case you're stuck at an intersection, you don't know where to go, you're despite everything battling with torment from long periods of being compelled to withdraw and rely upon others to show you your value, at that point right now is an ideal opportunity. How about we start your excursion towards the most joyful long periods of your life.

HOW TO GET THE MOST OUT OF THIS BOOK

This book is composed to work in various manners, for example,

- Read this book completely to guarantee that you completely comprehend the narcissist personality disorder, what causes this kind of turmoil, the signs and indications, casualties of narcissist misuse, and how to manage an individual with NPD or;

- Use the book as a manual for assist you with assessing and rehash bits of the book that you audit and rehash parts of the book that you may feel relates to you or somebody you know

- This book will assist you with understanding the impacts that the narcissistic personality disorder has on an individual when they need to manage this disorder in their family life, companions, colleague, a chief, or sentimental relationship.

- This book is composed to be enlightening and instructional. A portion of the data might be, for a few, staggering and may consider how somebody can get engaged with an individual with NPD who can be so pitiless and cheapen their very own individual contemplations and soul.

Be that as it may, when you peruse and comprehend what this narcissist disorder is about and how an individual can be pulled in and engage with an individual can be pulled in and engage with an individual with NPD, it will turn out to be increasingly under stable.

This book has been written with the expectation that you find out about individuals who have a narcissistic personality disorder and how one can have a superior comprehension of the turmoil, cheerful reading to you and yours!!

CHAPTER 1 – THE BASICS OF NARCISSISTIC ABUSE RECOVERY

You were convinced that it would be better for you. You believed you would feel free. You thought you would be able to take the pain. So why is it so difficult? Why does the hurt seem to have made a   home in your hear and your mind? Why do you feel even more trapped than ever?

Needless to say, healing from a narcissistic relationship might not follow the same process that other separations do. There are certain factors that can make it even harder for you, and that's why you might   feel   particularly at a loss in the months that follow your leaving. Understanding why it might be difficult can provide you valuable insight to   help   you realize that all these negative thoughts and feelings are temporary – they're nothing more than latent side-effects of the abuse that you've suffered all this time. The   sooner   you realize where they're stemming from, the sooner you'd be able to nip them at the   root and slowly release   yourself   from entanglement.

Why it's So Hard to Heal

Have you ever had to cut someone out   of your life before? Was it a toxic friend who just didn't jive with your personality? An absentee partner who just wasn't who you expected them to   be?   A competitive co-worker who saw every project as an opportunity to 'get ahead'?

While each of these scenarios might present varying inconveniences and challenges, one thing remains true–it probably didn't eat you up inside to say goodbye and walk away.

Sure, it's only normal that you might have felt the remnants of the relationship as your heart and mind worked to skip away the remaining ties that held you to this person. But once those few days or weeks had passed, you probably found yourself fully-functional once more. You might not have   even had to think about that person unless someone else brought them up.

You healed, you moved on, and you got better. It happened before, so why is it so hard now? There are unique aspects to a narcissistic relationship that makes it particularly difficult to cope with. So, after you walk away, you might find yourself feeling the same potent pain you did when they were still a part of your life.

So, what are these factors that make it so much harder?

The Narcissist's Grip

Perhaps a narcissist's most intricate and effective tool to keep their victims in line is their grip. This metaphorical grasp is slowly built over time, constructed with conditional love and affection that' later used as a tool to get you to act the way that they want you to.

As time wears on, the victim feels endeared to the narcissist, and the abuser will exploit this connection to their benefit. The victim becomes a scapegoat for all the different problems that might arise in the narcissist's life, even if the victim had no involvement in the development of the issue.

The narcissist now insists that you're problem, responsible for the different things that go wrong in your lives together. They convince you that you need them because you're not perfect, and they know what's best to keep you from maybe causing any more harm to yourself or to others. They make you believe that you rely on them, making you feel like you owe them an explanation or an apology

For every little thing that goes wrong.

You, on the other hand, are convinced. The kindness, affection, and 'love' that they showed you when your relationship was just beginning has convinced you that they have the best intentions. They've convinced you that they're 'superior' to everyone—including you— which makes them the only viable counsel and the only one who can provide you verified truth and advice.

Now, without you noticing, you've become entangled in their web. You feel reliant on them and the first question on your mind every single time you need to make a decision is "what would they think?" You're constantly walking on eggshells, careful not to do anything that would upset them, and striving to do everything to please them.

Unfortunately, simply leaving isn't enough to dismantle such a deep-seated mechanism. That's because as time wears on, this system will make you lose your sense of volition. Your reliance on the abuser becomes reflexive, and it becomes a challenge for you to make decisions on your own.

So now that you've left, you can't help but wonder what to do next. You feel the need to have someone tell you how to go about the process, and the only person you can think of is your abuser. Unfortunately, there isn't anyone else who will be able to help you through this time in your life as much as yourself.

The Feeling of Guilt

There is no such thing as a civil disengagement from a narcissistic relationship. So, it's probable that at this moment, you're not on speaking terms with your abuser. In fact, you might never be able to speak to them again. This is a reality that needs to be accepted.

Knowing that you're not on good terms with your abuser might cause feelings of guilt to kick in. They convinced you that anything amiss in your relationship was your fault, so now that you're indefinitely ignoring each other, you feel responsible for the situation.

This feeling of guilt can make you want to come crawling back, say you're sorry, and reclaim your place in their intricate mechanism. But going back and apologizing for something that isn't your fault will hardly fix anything, because you did nothing to apologize for in the first place.

Guilt plays such a big role in a failed recovery because it's often the reason why many victims end up rekindling ties with an abuser. Even allowing the guilt to just push you to reach out can be particularly dangerous because it gives the abuser the opportunity to shape the way you think and feel, making it more likely for you to engage once more.

The Lack of Support

It would be a lot easier to cope with narcissistic abuse if your family and friends could provide you support and insight. But because narcissists are what you might call great pretenders, they can effectively hide their true selves from anyone and everyone.

They spend their entire lifetime building an image of perfection and intelligence, establishing a character worthy of praise and admiration, even if their true life is far from perfect. This well-executed charade makes it impossible to have other people see the reality. Approaching friends and family who might know of your abuser will often lead to a dead end because they're not likely to believe what you have to say. After all, they've come to know the narcissist as the ideal individual, perhaps even a perfect person. So, they'll conclude that the things you're going through are probably just the fruits of misunderstanding.

For the most part, healing from a narcissist's abuse will have to be done on your own. Of course, there will always be support groups and online resources that you can leverage to find people with similar stories. But if you were expecting to gain the support of the people around you—especially if these people are also acquainted with the narcissist—then it might be impossible to receive their sympathy.

The Influence of Mainstream Media

Love conquers all, they say. Throughout the years, the media has taught us through books, movies, and music, that true love can set any mistake straight. We need to be selfless, to die to ourselves, to roll with the punches; we need to sacrifice our comfort and our convenience to show others that we love them.

So, whether it's a friend, a family member, or a romantic partner, the urge to keep fighting might be immensely strong because that's what we're taught to do. That's how we get our happy ending which is so often romanticized in majority of the films and songs we enjoy today. Unfortunately, there is a kind of fierce love and affection that the mainstream media fails to highlight, and that's self-love.

Often, when we tell others that we did something out of our desire to love ourselves, we're branded self-centred, inconsiderate, and selfish. We're not trying hard enough, and we're too lazy to give people love. We don't see other people's worth, and we don't put value on the long relationships we've established.

But before you allow those concepts any room in your mind, remember this – you are the most important person you have. So, don't let anyone invalidate your effort to care for yourself, especially if your abuser has done nothing to show that they're genuinely concerned for you. True enough, many of us are conditioned into acting like love-giving robots, able to dispense love and affection even in the most challenging emotional situations. But you can't pour from an empty vessel, and you definitely don't need to feel responsible for a relationship that'syou're solely trying to rescue.

Relationships are two-way streets, and they will never work out if there's only one person who's clocking in any time. Putting yourself before others isn't a selfish tactic; it's a mature way of dealing with things.

You can only truly care for someone if you're confident in your capacity to love which starts from within. In the same light, this kind of potent security in your being will attract the same kind of person, allowing a healthy, thriving relationship to grow without the pretences and ulterior motives.

The Unacknowledged Truth

Maybe you already spotted signs a while back. Maybe you already started to notice the strange behaviour. Maybe you chose to keep your mouth shut because you didn't want to start a fight. Maybe you turned a blind eye because that's not how you've come to know them. Whatever the case, you saw the signs, and you chose to ignore them.

Many of those who fall into the narcissist's trap can sense the problematic personality way before it even rears its ugly head. But they choose to sit silent and avoid confrontation because they want to believe in the best. They want to believe that this is a good person, and that these previews of strange behavior are nothing more than isolated instances.

Going against your gut and then finding out later that you were right about the way you felt can make it exceptionally difficult to move on. You'll find that the feeling of betraying your own radar can make you constantly want to beat yourself up and cry over the milk that you've spilled.

Although it can be frustrating, remember that everyone makes mistakes, and no one is exempted. While the repercussions of ignoring your gut might seem insurmountable especially because it trapped you in the narcissist's grasp, you need to understand that what you got out of the mistake was a learning experience. Not everyone gets to go through and survive such intense abuse, so you now have a unique chance to grow and mature, which many people don't get to have.

Don't beat yourself up over things that you no longer have control over. Instead, look forward to the future and learn to give your gut feeling due credit whenever it tips you off the next time around. You'd be surprised how well your intuition can keep you safe from a variety of threats around you, if you could only give it the attention it deserves.

Understanding the Truth about Narcissists

When you first heard, read, or learned the word 'narcissist', it might have been a light bulb moment. Wow—a word to define all those many years of abuse you suffered through. What a revelation.

Many of those abused by this type of person find it refreshing to be able to put a label on their abuser because it verifies their plight. These people exist and they are known to do exactly what was done to you. So even with everyone around you refusing to believe your story, you now feel somewhat vindicated.

Fortunately for you, this feeling isn't a onetime thing. Throughout your healing, you'll learn a world's worth of information that will feel like eureka moments, and they'll slowly show you the truth about your situation and the reality of the person you thought you knew.

During your recovery, it's highly encouraged that you continue to learn more about the narcissist archetype. Reading reliable resources and discovering the psychology behind their thinking will make it easier to put all the different experiences you had with them into context.

The more you learn, the easier it becomes for you to free yourself from the idea that you were wrong to leave. As you make more sense of their behavior, you'll soon discover that you never did anything wrong in the first place, and all the hurt, difficulties, and confusion you've dealt with for years can actually be traced back to their toxic personality.

Maintaining Your Distance

There is no tool more powerful than distance. Throughout your recovery process, you'll be confronted with the urge to turn back, make amends, and leave this rift behind you. But don't. No matter what you might think, no matter who might tell you to, no matter how hard it nags at your heart. You deserve your love more than anyone, especially more than someone who doesn't have your best interest in mind.

Maintaining your distance and refusing to speak with your abuser will give you enough white space to paint a picture of reality. Without that person there to reinforce the mechanisms in your head, you can wear them away and slowly but surely bring the entire machination to a stop, ultimately freeing yourself from their grip and attaining a new perspective on who you are and what you deserve.

In most cases, there will be no other people in your circle who will understand what it means to be abused by a narcissist. So, you'll often hear the same line over and over again: "people make mistakes, it's only right that you forgive them and give them a second chance."

While it is true that people make mistakes and most of them deserve second chances, narcissists are an exception to the rule. They will not change, they don't have insight, and they will never accept defeat. This means that for a relationship to be repaired, you need to be the one to try to fix it which only strengthens the narcissist's idea of unwavering correctness.

At the end of the day, you need to accept that reconciling is not an option. You might have to live the rest of your life without this person in the picture. And while that might be a bitter pill to swallow at any point in your healing, you need to know that it's for the best.

Loving yourself when you've been taught to put another person ahead every single time can be tough, but every journey starts with a single step. Understand that throughout this journey, you should be your focus. Keep your eyes and mind on the objective and don't forget why you're doing this in the first place. Your best life awaits.

CHAPTER 2 - THE NARCISSIST ARCHETYPE

No two people are the same. That's something we're taught as far back as elementary school. Back then, it was taken as nothing more than a quaint piece of truth, we are all different, and so we need to extend ourselves to understand one another so that the world becomes a happy place for everyone.

But as we grow older, we learn that that basic 'truth' might not actually be an accurate representation of reality. In fact, lots of people are the same in their behaviors, and this couldn't be any truer in the case of narcissists.

Considered 'psychopathic', narcissists are born of narcissists, making them act similarly across cultures, races, genders, and nationalities. They all think the same, and they all use the same tactics to abuse and malign those around them. That's why it's become easier for experts to pick out their qualities and spot them in a crowd, because they're predictable.

At this point in your recovery, you might find yourself asking questions about your abuser's personality. Understanding their motives and the reasons for certain tendencies they might have manifested can help you establish an accurate idea of who they really were. In the same way, knowing all the qualities of a narcissist can limit the chances of being abused again in the future.

THE SUBTLE SIGNS OF NARCISSISM

Narcissists operate covertly – that's why they're so hard to pinpoint. When you first met your abuser, you might have thought that they were a model citizen with their life perfectly put together. This initial image of perfection perhaps made you want to keep them near, marking the start of your abusive relationship.

Being subtle about their true tendencies helps draw in the victims. The more admirable they are, the more people will want to be in their good graces giving them enough narcissistic supply to feed their hungry egos. So it's possible that some of the signs of narcissism might completely fly over your head.

Here are some of the most common subtle signs of a narcissistic personality:

Not a Single Bad Shot

In our modern day and age, finding someone who isn't present on social media is like finding a unicorn. With the kind of convenience and access that social media platforms provide, it's become almost impractical for people to not use at least 2 of them.

Of course, your average everyday narcissist would take this as an opportunity to fire up their image and reinforce the charade they've so carefully crafted. In fact, studies have found that the commonality of narcissistic behaviors have risen since the dawn of social media, claiming that there might be a correlation between the two.

Essentially, social media works as a market where a narcissist can peddle him or herself to their sphere. Likes are the currency, and the more they get, the more satisfied they feel.

That's why they strive to create the perfect reflection of themselves on social media, often even lying about certain images of themselves to alter the context of the pictures and come up with a more pleasing post.

Scan through a narcissist's social media profile, and you're likely to notice 3 things. First, they won't have any bad pictures of themselves. Any and every image that includes them will have them looking particularly polished, garnering a hefty amount of likes and comments.

Second, you might notice that they often have perfect days every day. Every post is about a wonderful lunch with family, an intimate dinner with their significant other, a bird chirping on their windowsill in the morning, whatever might make their life look like it was ripped out of a Hallmark movie.

Third, they probably like to 'humble brag' about certain things in their life. For instance, one narcissistic mother posted a photo of a breakfast spread she had prepared with the caption "Labored over a hot stove to prepare this hearty meal for my son—the chief resident of the spinal surgery division at his hospital—who is coming over today!"

Obviously, the post was supposed to be about the breakfast she had made, but her caption shows you that she was merely taking the opportunity to talk about something else she found brag-worthy. Some will post images of certain things while slyly inserting other commodities to showcase their assets. In one case, a woman posted a photo of her freshly manicured nails by placing her hand against the steering wheel of her Audi's steering wheel.

In any case, a social media profile that seems too good to be true might be the facade for one narcissistic individual. Maintaining your distance from them and avoiding feeding into the hype by withholding likes and comments will make you less vulnerable to their trap.

Aversion to Correction

Narcissists have an incessant need to be correct and will fight tooth and nail to make sure they have the last say in any situation, even when they're talking to an expert. At the start, it might not be as pronounced, but you will notice hints of their aversion to correction in small however consistent instances.

A Loud Voice That Demands to Be Heard

Have you ever tried having a casual conversation with a narcissist? Rarely do they take the form of a 'conversation'. Talking with a narcissist might seem more like simply listening to one since they might not give you the space to say your piece.

With an ingrained sense of correctness and superiority, narcissists believe that the only opinions and ideas that matter are their own. Any contributions from anyone else are inferior and faulty, even if they're logically sound. Of course, that's not something a narcissist will ever come to realize given the fact that they won't even give other contributors the light of day.

Something you'll notice frequently with a narcissist is that they have the tendency to speak over others. Even during casual conversation, they take the opportunity to dominate, giving others very little chance to interject. In this way, the conversation can be steered in a direction that serves their own benefit.

That's why on many occasions, you'll find that a conversation with a narcissist becomes nothing more than a speech about him or herself.

The Need to Please and Flatter

There's something charming about a narcissist, that's how they reel in their victims. Knowing full well that they need to feed off the admiration and praise that others provide them, narcissists have a way of drawing in unsuspecting victims to turn into their narcissistic supply.

As your relationship develops, they feed your own narcissistic tendencies, which are present in all of us, however not full blown. What happens is that we see this perfect person and we end up wanting to be near them so that others associate us with this ideal individual.

It's like our adolescent longing to become best friends with the most popular kid in school. The rationalization is that if we're associated with this perfect person, then some of their ideal traits might rub off on us.

Now, the narcissist knows what you're trying to do, and they will feed your desire to become like them. So, they treat you like an extension, telling you you're doing a great job, making you feel important, and giving you validation that's rarely given to others. This makes you feel worthy and proud, making you hunger for that kind of attention.

So, what you do is you find ways to please them, you do things simply to make the narcissist happy, and you strive to maintain your status as their right-hand guy or gal. Soon enough, you'll find that most of your actions and choices are patterned around their preferences or desires.

If you're starting to notice that you're becoming too invested in receiving validation from someone else, check yourself. If anything, the only validation worth striving for is your own. While it might feel nice to receive it from others, learning to accept yourself and being happy with the way you are is far more important than any acceptance you might receive from external sources.

Narcissistic Behavior Patterns

A 'psychopath' is defined as a person suffering from mental disorder, who may manifest abnormal or violent social behavior. They are considered unstable and aggressive, allowing them to cause significant emotional, mental, and in some extreme cases, even physical abuse on those around them.

While it might come as a surprise to you, it's

important that you know that your narcissistic abuser is a psychopath. These people have very deep-seated mental issues with roots that reach as far back as their early childhood. That's why it's impossible to help a narcissist to recovery.

In-depth studies of psychopathic and narcissistic behavior have revealed behavioral patterns that they typically follow. These tendencies are present in almost all narcissists, and many of them manifest the same personalities although to varying degrees.

Keep in mind that although we all have narcissistic tendencies, not everyone showcases them to the point of being labeled a psychopath. Only when these behaviors cause abnormalities in social functioning is the person then considered a full blown, malignant narcissist.

Gas lighting

Gas lighting is a term that originates from a movie of the same title which was released in 1944. This term refers to a tactic used by certain individuals— especially narcissists—in an attempt to sow seeds of doubt into a specific individual.

The method of gas lighting changes depending on the situation, but the objective is always the same; to reinvent the past so that their previous mistakes or errors are not brought to light.

Smear Campaign

Wondering why people might start to distance themselves from you after you cut ties with a narcissist? You can probably thank their smear campaign tactics for the sudden loss of friends. Although smear campaigns are more popular in the realm of politics, narcissists have been known to use similar strategies. Once you break it off with a narcissist, one thing would have become apparent to them – you're aware of their true nature. This means if you decide to expose the narcissist for what they truly are— which might not even be on your agenda —then they may have to watch as their carefully constructed persona starts burning to the ground. Now this isn't something they're willing to risk.

So, what do they do? They use smear campaigns to remain one step ahead.

Using what information they have about you and your relationship, they'll make the move to talk to mutual friends and connections to clarify why you're no longer on speaking terms. This may involve tweaking certain events and information in order to make you look like a horrible person.

It's worth mentioning that a narcissist won't simply settle for saying a few nasty things about you. They want to completely dismantle your credibility and reputation. This way, they can be sure that you'd have a hard time trying to convince people of your side not only because you'd seem unreliable, but also because your friends and contacts would likely choose to avoid you all together.

A narcissist's smear campaign can leave you with no one else but yourself. Some rumors and gossip can be so horrible that it may even jeopardize your job and your intimate relationships. Remember, they probably never really cared about you in the first place, so don't be surprised if they suddenly turn into someone completely unrecognizable and start spewing absolute lies about who you are and what you've done. Abuse by Proxy

If there's one thing a narcissist will have an endless supply of, it's people. Their charm and seeming perfection just makes others gravitate towards them, the same way you probably clung to your abuser when you first met them.
Unfortunately, anyone who tries to cross a narcissist will find him or herself dealing with the onslaught of the rest of the posse.
This is what you might call abuse by proxy. The process starts when you displease a narcissist. Their need to shame and discourage you will kick in, and they'll make sure you feel how unhappy they are with what you've done. But they'll often go the extra mile and make sure to

hit you where it hurts. That' where their people step in.

A narcissist will talk negatively about you to other people in your circle. They'll convince these individuals that you're gravely at fault, and that you need to be taught a lesson. What's interesting is that they often won't give such obvious instructions. The tactic more closely resembles brainwashing, making other people believe certain lies and encouraging them to act on these ideas without actually giving them overt instructions.

Conditional love is another well-used tool in the narcissistic arsenal. This method provides the victim with just enough affection to feed their desire to be on the narcissist's good side, making them feel worthy and sufficient for the time being. Narcissists will often pull out this tactic when the victim pleases them or does anything to benefit them, working as positive reinforcement that makes the victim want to continue to do good.

Unfortunately, love that qualifies as genuine love should have to be unconditional. That is, it doesn't choose when to love, but rather chooses to love despite the person's shortcomings. This is sadly not something that the narcissist is capable of.

If the victim does anything that goes against their desires, preferences, or ideas, the narcissist simply withholds love and affection, making the victim feel unworthy and undeserving of the narcissist's care. It's only when an apology and an acknowledgment of the wrongdoing will the narcissist 'forgive' the victim.

By choosing when to give love and when to withhold it, the narcissist effectively keeps the victim in line. No one wants to get on a narcissist's bad side, especially because their approval is so highly valued.

Finally, it's important to talk about how a narcissist might blame you for everything. This tactic keeps their image clean and blemish-free while causing their victim to develop a concept of accountability. Abusers don't want to be wrong in any situation, and so they exercise every opportunity to make sure that they don't get blamed for any bad publicity.

They find a scapegoat—often their current victim—and they turn any and every situation around to make the person feel bad about him or herself. This in effect makes the victim feel unworthy, causing them to cling even tighter to the abuser in fear of being left.

In many cases, narcissists will also let other people know of the victim's failures.

This is done overtly, with the scapegoat fully aware that other individuals in their sphere are aware of their 'mistakes'. This instills embarrassment, and makes the victim submit completely to the abuser to show remorse and a willingness to set themselves straight.

All of these manipulation strategies don't only make the victim act a certain way now, they also instill a long-term mechanism that keeps the relationship the way it is for the foreseeable future. Breaking down the victim's free-will and sense of self-worth makes them reliant on the abuser, allowing the narcissist to control the victim's thoughts and actions. What's the purpose of control, you ask? Simple – narcissists thrive on admiration and praise. Having you under their spell makes it possible for them to have a narcissistic supply whenever they need it. A victim's endless longing to please and appease the narcissist gives the abuser a consistent resource for admiration.

On top of that, they feel like their superiority entitles them to put others under them. In their minds, they're the best and that means they have the right to belittle others and make them subordinates in whatever way possible. By taking control of your life and decisions, they feel they're doing you a favor since they believe they know better than everyone else.

Spotting a Narcissist in the Real World

Having trouble figuring out who just might be a narcissist? They can be difficult to spot because they're so good at concealing their truth. At the start, they're likely to appear very likeable and well-rounded, making those around them gravitate towards them. It's only when you fall too deep into their trap that it becomes apparent what they truly are.

There are a few markers you can use to help identify them in the real world.

Often, these tell-tale signals should manifest all together, allowing you to identify the narcissist with more accuracy.

A Pleasing Personality

Narcissists have a knack for making themselves look exceptionally flawless to the public. They're friendly, smiley, and charming, making new acquaintances feel comfortable in their familiar and amiable aura. They tend to make you feel good about yourself even right off the bat which might cause you to think that they genuinely like you, too.

They will draw attention towards themselves by talking about their most esteemed accomplishments, which may endear you to them even more. The idea that this person is friendly and successful makes them even more admirable.

Essentially, their entire persona makes you want to be their friend, be close to them, and be associated with them in whatever little way possible.

This is because we as humans have a natural tendency to think that associating with successful, smart, beautiful, or 'ideal' people will somehow uplift our own image. That's why many of us probably struggled to rub elbows with the coolest kids in school.

A good way to pick out a narcissist would be to assess their persona and how well you know them. Is there any bad news about who they are? Have you heard any stories that talk about any possible negative things they've done or said? Or are they completely polished and blemish-free? If you notice that a person seems too good to be true, they probably are.

...Only When It's Necessary

There are what you might call 'levels' of worth in a narcissist's mind. People who obviously have more money, success, or are considered more physically appealing are acknowledged as 'superior' in a narcissist's mind, so these people obviously receive the best treatment narcissists have to offer. People who fall within the same financial, success, and beauty bracket are considered equals and are treated the same. Those who fall slightly below the narcissist's self-appraisal are still deserving of praise and good treatment, but they're awarded on a conditional basis. That is, these people need to do something in order to deserve the narcissist's approval and praise.

Finally, there are people of zero interest to the narcissist. These are average everyday individuals who are seen as unnecessary and irrelevant, so narcissists won't bother being nice or spending effort to show their good side.

CHAPTER 3: NARCISSISTIC PERSONALITY DISORDER (NPD)

General Personality

The expression "narcissism" has its foundations in Greek folklore, Narcissus, as indicated by legend, was so pulled in by her magnificence as reflected in the water to fall into it and suffocate, as per another variant of the fantasy, he was devoured by melancholy at not having the option to arrive at his darling appearance in the water, until he passed on, and rather than his body from his blood a blossom was conceived, which was called Narcissus. The fundamental element of Narcissistic Personality Disorder is an image of the pattern to prevalence, requirement for profound respect, and absence of affectability to other people. People with narcissistic disorder have, for more often than not, a high self-respect. They routinely overstate their aptitudes, frequently seeming pompous. They believe they're extraordinary, prevalent, must be fulfilled in each solicitation and qualified for exceptional treatment.

Expect that others perceive their status as unique individuals and, if this occurs, they admire. Alternately, if the others are scrutinizing their quality respond with outrage, being unequipped for addressing and acknowledge analysis. People with narcissistic personality disorder normally experience disorders perceiving that others have wants, emotions and necessities. They accept that their needs precede all things, and that their method for seeing things is the main right one around the world, demonstrating impassion from the perspective of others and powerlessness to get him. Along these lines, for instance, people with narcissistic disorder can hope to abstain from lining and being served quickly dedicated and servers. Regardless, regardless of whether the case is over so irritated when they wind up meeting the desires, shared standards, envious of not having their needs met right away.

Relational relations are along these lines ordinarily undermined due to disorders emerging from over the top requests, the requirement for esteem, and the relative negligence for the sentiments of others.

Narcissistic people, at that point, are frequently jealous of others or accepts that others are desirous of them. They will in general observe others in key serious and endeavour to build up and keep up a place of matchless quality. All the time, in the high places of any chain of importance (corporate, institutional, and so forth.), we discover individuals with narcissistic personality, as their characteristics are useful in the challenge at work. They get magnificent outcomes without acknowledging what number of individuals do the expenses of their demeanours or stay harmed by them. Relational connections are coming up short.

Pick accomplices by and large feeble and agreeable, who appreciate them and cause them to feel significant. Sooner or later 'time, in any case, they are exhausted, they feel disappointed and go looking for new tease, intended to invigorate them once more, or attempt to turn/your accomplice and debased it exactly as they would prefer. Indeed, even infatuated live with a consistent feeling of rivalry and the taste that draw from the report, mainly that of the victory of the "prey".

Live sexual relations with a solid exhibition nervousness, which now and again makes them a casualty of sexual brokenness, which for them are a catastrophe. In the uncommon situations when they go into an association with an individual "at their level", which doesn't appreciate them, to which they are to stick truly experience the ill effects of high tension of surrender and, on account of a crack, give in to sadness. Same destiny occurs for them on the off chance that they get substantial disappointments at work or losing a significant challenge. Regardless, narcissists, in any event, when they believe they have all that they need (achievement, love, cash, and so forth.). Continually feel unsatisfied and experience phases of sadness which can't give a clarification.

The principle highlight of the narcissistic personality disorder comprises in the inclination to respond protectively when the individual feels an injury to its worth. Accordingly it is simple for individuals to embrace frames of mind haughty, self-important, disdain others and discovers them the reason for his disorders. People who have this disorder accept they are uncommon and novel individuals. They hope to get endorsement and applause for their predominant quality, being stunned when they don't get the acknowledgment they think they merit and regularly exhibiting the inclination to ruminate about the disappointment with respect to the next.

Together with this, we find in them the propensity to respond to analysis encountering outrage from one viewpoint, the other disgrace.

By temperance of the individual worth that accept they have, these individuals expect they need to visit and can be seen uniquely by uncommon individuals, renowned or high social or scholarly, from the thought that their needs are outside the ability to comprehend and the capability of customary individuals. Requires over the top reverence from the earth. Have the desire that everything is because of them and that, because of their being extraordinary individuals or more, must acquire ideal treatment, just as the prompt fulfilment of their needs, which they expect others fundamentally subject themselves, and when this isn't happens, they become irate and cavalier. This feeling of qualification, together with the absence of affectability to the wants and needs of others, frequently bring about a propensity to misuse and control relational people who have a narcissistic personality disorder, truth be told, will in general structure fellowships or sentimental connections just in the event that they realize that the other can help fulfil their own motivations (as a matter of first importance fortify and improve confidence and self-esteem); anticipate likewise immense accessibility and commitment with respect to other people, to manhandle, without respect for the outcomes. Corresponding to this, the other is glorified up to that fulfils the requirement for esteem and delight, for then additionally be strongly debased when never again plays out this capacity.

These people for the most part need compassion, demonstrating incapable to perceive the sentiments and requirements of others and to relate to them. At the point when the abstract understanding of the other is refined, it is by and large imagined disparagingly, as an indication of shortcoming and absence of self-esteem. As a rule, be that as it may, over the span of treatment, when the restorative relationship has been built up show to have profoundly created abilities additionally depict the mental existence of the individuals in their neighbourhood.

Seeing someone will in general show up genuinely cold and isolates, and paying little heed to the torment that create another in view of their perceptions and contemplations, frequently communicated in tones haughty and disdainful. The hole is highlighted when others feel penniless or go to them for help. At long last, they are regularly caught up in dreams of boundless achievement, power, splendour, excellence, or perfect love, jealous of others or accept that others are desirous of them. By and large will in general jealousy to different triumphs and properties, accepting that he merits a greater amount of them the outcomes they have accomplished or benefits they appreciate right now, to debase the commitments of others at whatever point they get acknowledgment or thankfulness for their work.

The narcissistic personality disorder has its beginning in early adulthood. The narcissistic qualities can be very normal in youths, yet not really show that in adulthood the individual will confront a narcissistic personality disorder. The individuals who experience the ill effects of this disorder may likewise exhibit significant troubles in adjusting to the beginning of physical confinements and/or business related to the maturing procedure. Roughly 5075% of people who have been determined to have narcissistic personality disorder are male. Appraisals of the predominance of this disorder shift from 2% to 16% in clinical populace and are under 1% in the overall public.

Regularly people who have a narcissistic personality disorder embrace a psychotherapeutic treatment in time they create burdensome states which are never again ready to help. The activating variables of this downturn will in general comprise of hazardous connections or breaking them, by bombing matches in the expert circle, a feeling of disappointment with their lives, from misfortunes or disappointments that reduce the feeling of glory, producing from one viewpoint demoralization, thrashing and disappointment, the other disgrace and embarrassment.

At the base of narcissistic despondency features the impression of a significant disparity between admired desires and reality, right now, was an attention on the beliefs of thought disappointed and baffled self-important desires and the cut-off points of the earth to help and empower the formation of what was normal. This condition delivers an attending feeling of hopelessness, connected from one perspective to the end that "things are rarely truly well, and the fantasies won't work out as expected ever," the avoidance of other social contacts, all together not to uncover themselves on appraisals negative about their state of torment. Notwithstanding these burdensome states, has recognized the presence of other manifestation pictures or social disorders that can cause people with narcissistic personality disorder to take part in psychotherapy.

In particular, it was discovered that they may wish to stop the inconvenience of co-happening disorder, for example, social uneasiness, neurosis, or maltreatment of psychoactive substances and liquor. Excessive touchiness to the judgment, mostly as high worry for supposed deformities in the picture and execution, can get show in circumstances of social nervousness, discovering its definitive articulation when these people look for the consideration of ' condition and simultaneously, they dread the objection. In hypochondriasis, the emphasis on the consideration of your body gives a socially worthy approach to concentrate and time on themselves, getting the comprehension and thought of nature, simultaneously, the powerlessness or physical constraints may comprise a defence for the disappointment of the pretentious desires.

The maltreatment of psychoactive substances and liquor, at long last, creates a profound positive feeling from individual misery, and in like manner, the utilization of them permits the accomplishment of conditions of loftiness and force. By and large, the conviction that they have remarkable capacities requirement for these people to abstain from conceding their dependence on medications or liquor, persuading that they can get away from the antagonistic impacts of fixation itself, intruding on use when the desire. Thus, at times, people with a narcissistic personality disorder can take a psychotherapeutic treatment from a condition of profound indignation, which now and then appears as provocation and hostility, both verbal and physical, towards the other saw as incapacitating.

This condition is identified with neurotic propensities, which are communicated through the conviction "me against the world", beginning with the evaluation that the others, jealous of their prevalence, are set on harming or loathing them, along these lines representing a risk to their confidence and their own worth. In such conditions, the propensity of these people is from one viewpoint to provide for others the obligation regarding their disappointments, the other to actualize enthusiastic practices, which allure or overwork, so as to solidify its predominance and its capacity. In spite of the fact that the degree of enduring experienced by these people is regularly extensively higher, the conviction that "the individuals who are sick is feeble and who is frail is judged adversely and agreeable" keeps them from looking for help and straightforwardly express their inconvenience with the aftereffect of incite them to receive frames of mind characterized by a significant separation from the disorders announced. On this point likewise influences the trouble, specifically those experiencing narcissistic personality disorder, access to their inner states, distinguishing and perceiving one's own feelings, needs and wants, and the discourse of the narcissist is regularly dynamic and hypothetical, not focused on the account scenes of life.

At the point when people with narcissistic personality disorder are in such a state, they experience a significant feeling of vacancy devitalized, in which passionate experience is dull and contacts social maintained a strategic distance from. It is a condition that isn't depicted as disagreeable despite what might be expected, these individuals stay long right now which, "in the shut casing" and "distant"

Confidence and mental self-view are focal in people who have a narcissistic personality disorder: they have a lopsidedly constructive self-observation, however behind an exterior haughty, shroud a feeling of shortcoming and insufficiency, just as a low confidence self, which is "uncovered" each time the earth doesn't give the profound respect and endorsement desires. Be that as it may, while getting to the impression of individual trouble or shortcoming don't hope to be helped - and in this manner barely request a psychotherapy - yet be agreeable. Rather, they keep an eye on self-defensive confinement.

CHAPTER 4: DIAGNOSTIC CRITERIA IN NARCISSISTIC & NARCISCISM

The Diagnostic and Statistical Manual of Mental Disorders, Fourth Edition (American Psychiatric Association, 1994) describes Narcissistic Personality Disorder as a pervasive pattern of grandiosity (in fantasy or behaviour), need for admiration, and lack of empathy , which begins in early adulthood and is present in a variety of contexts, as indicated by five (or more) of the following:

- ✓ Has a grandiose sense of self-importance (e.g., exaggerates achievements and talents, expects to be recognized as superior without commensurate achievements);
- ✓ Is preoccupied with fantasies of success, power, brilliance, beauty unlimited, or ideal love;
- ✓ Believes that he or she is "special" and unique and can only be understood by, or

should associate with, other people (or institutions) special or high-status;

✓ Requires excessive admiration;

✓ He has a sense of entitlement, i.e., unreasonable expectations of especially favourable treatment or automatic compliance with his expectations;

✓ Interpersonally exploitive, i.e., takes advantage of others to achieve his goals;

✓ Lacks empathy: is unwilling to recognize or identify with the feelings and needs of others;

✓ Is often envious of others or believes that others are envious of him or her; - Shows arrogant, haughty behaviours or attitudes.

The Dimensional Perspective

Here is a hypothetical profile, in terms of the five-factor model of personality, for narcissistic personality disorder. - High neurosis

Chronic negative effects, including anxiety, fear, tension, irritability, anger, dejection, hopelessness, guilt, shame, difficulty in inhibiting impulses: for example, to eat, drink, or spend money, irrational beliefs, for example, unrealistic expectations, questions perfectionistic self, unwarranted pessimism unfounded somatic concerns, helplessness and dependence on others for emotional support and decision making.

- **High Extraversion**

Trend Excessive talking, leading to inappropriate and social friction, inability to spend time alone, attention seeking and overly dramatic expression of emotions, excitement seeking unbridled inappropriate attempts to dominate and control others.

- **Low Openness**

Difficulty adapting to social or personal change, low tolerance or understanding of different points of view or different lifestyles, emotional blandness and inability to understand and verbalize own feelings; alexithymia; constricted range of interests, insensitivity to art and beauty, excessive conformity to authority.

- **Ability to low agreement**

Cynicism and paranoid thinking, inability to trust even friends or family, litigation, too ready to pick fights; exploitive and manipulative; lying; rude and inconsiderate manner alienates friends, limits social support, lack of respect for social conventions can lead to problems with the law, inflated and grandiose sense of self; arrogance.

- **Conscientiousness low**

Low results: not fulfilling the intellectual or artistic potential; poor academic performance relative to ability; disregard of rules and responsibilities can 'lead to trouble with the law, unable to discipline self (e.g., stick to diet or program exercise) even when required for medical reasons, lack of personal and occupational aimlessness.

Basic creed: I am special. Strategy: Self-aggrandizement. In Cognitive therapy of personality disorders, lists the typical beliefs associated with each specific personality disorder. Here are some of the typical beliefs.

- Since they are superior, I am entitled to special treatment and privileges.

- I must not be bound by the rules that apply to other people.

- If others do not respect my status, should be punished.

- Other people should satisfy my needs.

- Other people should recognize how special I am.

- Since I have so much talent, the others must be done in four to promote my career.

- The need for anyone else to interfere with mine.

According to data reported by the American Psychiatric Association (APA), the narcissistic personality disorder is diagnosed in about 1% of the adult population. However, there are higher estimates, which put the figure between 2% and 4%. Among patients hospitalized the spread of the disorder increases enormously (between 2% and 16%). The spread of this disease does not seem ubiquitous, but strongly influenced - at least in the mode of manifestation - from cultural contexts. According to some observers, it is rife with these features almost exclusively in Western capitalist countries.

The disorder appears to have a sexual component or gender to which the distribution is not equal between the sexes: the male patients outnumber women, a share of between 50% and 75%. Some narcissistic traits appear during the development of the individual and to a certain degree is normal. These personality traits are widespread among adolescents and teenagers, not necessarily the outcome is a pathological personality in adulthood.

The Narcissistic Personality Disorder appears in the DSM-IV TR between personality disorders group B. The APA is planning to eliminate the narcissistic personality disorder in the DSM V: believes that narcissism is not a disease in itself, but a disorder that can be spread on different diagnostic pictures, so much so that we have only one type of narcissism but different. But apart from considering the pros and cons of this decision of the APA, one thing remains well-founded: the best therapy for the Narcissistic Personality Disorder continues to be that analytical.

For there to be diagnosed with narcissistic personality disorder, the DSM-IV-TR requires that you meet certain diagnostic criteria, from which emerges the figure of a person with narcissistic personality disorder tends to arrogance, intrusiveness, our desire to be always the centre of attention. Glen O. Gab bard noted, however, as the Narcissistic Personality Disorder is subject to many nuances: the narcissist we reserved, so sensitive to rejection fear constantly, including avoiding being the centre of attention, there is the greedy identified by Kornberg and to Kohut, constantly at risk of fragmentation of the self. According to Gab bard, the narcissistic personality disorder swings between two poles ranging from unconscious narcissism (in which the person is not aware of the reaction that creates in others, maintaining an apparent superiority over the idea that the world can hurt him), narcissism hyper vigilant (in which the person is extremely sensitive to the reactions of others, try shame easily and just as easily humiliated, while paying the utmost attention to the movements of the other to identify and highlight flaws and lack of respect).

The main "signs" of a narcissistic personality disorder are:

- ➤ Believe that people do not appreciate their talents and their high quality special;
- ➤ The idea that in one's life does not add up, for example, have been less successful than expected, or in spite of personal

achievements, however, feel a sense of emptiness, apathy and boredom;

➤ Consider extremely important to receive the attention and admiration of others

➤ Believe that everything is due: claim, without reason, to receive a particular treatment or favour that their requests are necessarily satisfied;

➤ Tend to hide their difficulties;

➤ Feel a sense of emotional distance in the relationship, or give them little importance or feel your partner a figure accessory in their own lives;

➤ Flaunt behaviours or attitudes arrogant and conceited.

Numerous individuals may have narcissistic personality qualities, be that as it may, just when these characteristics are resolute, maladaptive and steady, causing a considerable debilitation of the working of the individual and a huge abstract torment, at that point they establish a narcissistic personality disorder. Together with this, beginning from the perception that it is conceivable to distinguish the nearness of these highlights in other mental disorder, it is suitable to feature some major differentiations between narcissistic personality disorder and different conditions that may appear to be externally comparative. Both the narcissistic personality disorder in that fanatical enthusiastic personality disorder are featured goal for flawlessness and the inclination to accept that others are not ready to get things done just as for the subject makes.

These disarranges contrast, be that as it may, in that, while subjects with over the top urgent personality disorder are normally self-basic and disappointed with the outcomes accomplished, people with narcissistic personality disorder are bound to accept that they have arrived at the standard which they strive for stickler. Despite the fact that the propensity to hair-splitting additionally characters anorexia nervosa, it is to be recognized from a similar element in the narcissistic personality disorder, since it is obvious basically inside a structure ruled by the worry for the weight and picture body. The two patients with narcissistic personality disorder than those with avoidant personality disorder are inclined to encountering sentiments of disgrace.

The contrast between them lies in the way that subjects who have a narcissistic personality disorder all the more effectively arrive at states they see higher and, in this manner, shielded from such feelings; Moreover, while they glancing in different affirmations to its pretentiousness, subjects with avoidant personality disorder rather try to give his very own false representation deficiency. The general soundness of mental self-view, just as the overall nonappearance of reckless and imprudent lead, and worry for the relinquishment, for recognizing the narcissistic personality disorder from marginal personality disorder, despite the fact that they share a propensity to responses outrage notwithstanding passionate boosts additionally insignificant.

Correspondingly, inordinate pride in the accomplishments, the propensity to dismissal for the shortcomings of others and, most importantly, an overall absence of passionate indications, can be recognized from the narcissistic personality disorder Histrionic Personality Disorder, despite the fact that they share the need of consideration all things considered. Right now, people with narcissistic disorder, marginal personality disorder and Histrionic Personality Disorder show the capacity to take unnecessary considerations, those with narcissistic personality disorder explicitly require to be respected for their uncommon characteristics, while those with BPD and Histrionic personality are all the more ready to seem frail and poor, if this permits them to get consideration. Individuals with narcissistic personality disorder share with introverted personality disorder will in general effectively exploit relational relations, demonstrating shallow and profoundly sympathetic.

Simultaneously, the narcissistic personality disorder does exclude parts of impulsivity, animosity and unscrupulousness, likewise, people with narcissistic personality disorder normally don't have a background marked by direct disorder in youth or criminal conduct in adulthood. People with solitary personality disorder may at last not be as destitute of reverence and desirous of others just as results being ordinary in people with narcissistic personality disorder.

Suspiciousness and social withdrawal recognize people with a jumpy disorder or schizotypal personality disorder from those with a narcissistic personality disorder:

When these characteristics are apparent in patients with narcissistic personality disorder, they will in general originate from the dread that they might be found imperfections or deformities in their own picture. The greatness that characterizes narcissistic personality disorder can without much of a stretch rise in hyper or hypomanic scenes, which were commonplace state of mind of bipolar disorder, however the relationship with temperament unsettling influence and utilitarian debilitation recognizing these scenes from narcissistic personality disorder. At last, this disorder must be recognized from a personality change because of a general ailment, where the qualities develop because of the immediate impacts of a general ailment on the Central Nervous System.

It ought to likewise be recognized additionally by side effects that may create in relationship with the incessant utilization of substances (such as, on account of the turmoil identified with cocaine).

CHAPTER 5: ETIOLOGY IN NPD

As per Freud, the individual is driven by two parts instinctual moxie, seen as indispensable and innovative clairvoyant vitality and the passing sense. His hypothesis of libidinal improvement gives a degree of sensuality, called narcissistic or essential narcissism, in which the individual himself is the object of their libidinal drives, trailed by a phase known as the "object decision" in which the drives are fulfilling in an article outside the person. At the phase of essential narcissism, the drives are a first appropriate article agreeable to them, however this thing isn't outside to the individual, yet is your "I" itself, which starts to come to fruition around then. Right now won't surrender never completely: a specific measure of moxie, and will remain perpetually in the self-image itself determine the accompanying decisions by object of sexual motivations. Highlight of the arena is the narcissistic power that originates from the way that the individual drives are in a similar subject their "source" and their "object", without the need to look for fulfilment outside.

In grown-up life, in circumstances of prejudice to the dissatisfactions of the real world, there might be a relapse to this period of libidinal improvement that prompts a phase of auxiliary narcissism neurotic characteristic of narcissistic depression or schizophrenia, where the common powerlessness to utilize the libidinal, the crucial vitality in the enthusiastic connections that are so troublesome and dangerous. As per another creator, neurotic narcissism has an alternate birthplace. Around 3-5 years the kid is regularly ready to coordinate reasonable pictures of good and awful self and outer items in mental portrayals reliable and stable future narcissistic subject, in any case, doesn't have this capacity, and looks to unite the positive and admired portrayals, both self and article, consequently shaping an obsessive pretentious self, a thought that is unreasonable and romanticized self. This contorted picture of himself, obviously, is kept up that the narcissist is consistently needing outer fortifications for his confidence and is dependent upon nonstop disillusionments.

That which favours the arrangement of this neurotic affected self might be the frame of mind of parent's cool, confined, and yet loaded with misrepresented deference and desires for the youngster. Various examinations recommend the significance of hereditary effect on the advancement of narcissistic character issue.

In particular, they show the presence of an inherited transmission of 45% comparative with commonplace parts of narcissistic consideration chasing, the should be complimented and greatness. Different examinations propose that, in the advancement of narcissistic character issue, involves a position of essential significance is the connection that creates between the parent and the kid, specifically, the individuals who have this issue appear to have created from the association with their folks, connections characterized for the most part by a portrayal of themselves as needing care and a portrayal of others like that are not accessible to give it, at that point the desire for being dismissed. This condition brings about the subject will in general sort out their lives by getting rid of the affection for other people and doesn't need their help, depending just on itself and looking for supreme independence, not perceiving and communicating their needs, taking frames of mind of separation and predominance. Beginning from this reason, the closeness is taking steps to set up a region as far as waste, for which the individual before long figures out how to give up it.

Simultaneously, since the connection figure is seen as separating and out of reach, not show the requirement for it gives off an impression of being the most ideal approach to have the option to accomplish a specific portion of closeness against it; together with this, the subject creates from one hand, the inclination to separate apparent as negative parts of oneself (wants and shortcomings) as uncover the further danger of being dismissed, the other a propensity to embrace dispositions that make conceivable the most agreeable according to the connection figure same. Now, the subject builds up the conviction that closeness to another ought to be forced or pressured by tight control, in this way meaning to have the other, as opposed to be with him, realizing that it would not acknowledge it always, being unable to pick.

Corresponding to this, in a relationship wherein the subject has the feeling that the other isn't there (or on the grounds that it is really missing, far off, unengaged or in light of the fact that it is truly present, however unfit to offer notice to his needs) , you become acclimated to consider his universe of importance as the one existing right now, the negations from outside is separated and not thought about, with the goal that the individual builds up a propensity to an incredible portrayal of self, ' desire for reserving the privilege to get unique treatment, the demeanour to forceful frames of mind towards a situation that doesn't live up to your desires.

Perceptions on the early parent-kid cooperation's likewise recommend the nearness of a style of care where the kid is considered by the parent as a "medium" through which to create and improve confidence, never to be acknowledged for their ability and all alone merits. In spite of the fact that the family condition of the individual with narcissistic character issue may appear to be well disposed towards the last mentioned, truth be told, the parental figures are commonly without compassion, genuinely cold and separated, profoundly unfit to address the issues of the kid and right now happens that they credit to their kids jobs or capacities that are wrong to the individuals who are their ordinary developmental procedures. In such conditions, the passionate hardship by parental figures is by all accounts the premise of the demeanour out of control that more often than not people with narcissistic character issue will in general accept in social circle.

Seems relevant also come from a family considered by most of the community as different on the basis of ethnic, racial, geographical or economic status. In such situations, the concept of self is to be characterized by feelings of inadequacy and inferiority, envy, from the refuge in fantasies idealized attachment to people or prestige. The families of narcissists are frequently isolated from a social point of view, why the future narcissist, not developed the ability to recognize the commonality and group membership, addresses the threat to self-esteem invoking the sense of superiority and belief of be "excluded because envied."

In psychology, the history of narcissism is usually traced back to Freud with his work of 1914 "Introduction (Einführung) to narcissism." This study, as Freud himself recognizes, in a letter to Abraham: born bad "narcissism was a hard work and bring all signs of its deformity." Written very quickly because aimed at countering criticism of Jung about not being able to apply the libido theory to explain the schizophrenic psychosis, has clear inconsistency. However, we must not overlook the fact that with this work, Freud tries to set up a comprehensive theory of psychic development of man. And this explains the persistence of this disorder, despite the uncertain and fragile initial theory. The fundamental "aporia", that long will weigh in the development of thought psychoanalytical and not only is the concept of primary narcissism that proposes and absolutists the vision of the search object as drive discharge, with the consequent denial of the importance of the object and the external reality.

The denial of the importance of external reality, which began in 1897, will be in this phase, the extreme monadic conception of man. The child at birth would tend only to maintain, through discharge of impulses, a situation of peaceful indifference (nirvana). If we compare this concept with the famous statement, certainly provocative, of Winnicott "There is the child" we can understand the long process needed to pass the Freudian statement about man's nature, but we are now in 1960. Already in the 40s, however, W. D.

Fairbairn, had begun to question the assumption Freudian, offering a completely different view. For Fairbairn purpose of the libido is always and only the research object. Everyone, from birth, is looking for an emotional-affective. This intentionality he calls libido, it connotes a new property: desire.

But the desire may not always be welcomed and satisfied if there is a chronic emotional unavailability of the mother, while the libidinal ego tends to languish, there is an anti-libidinal which is the result of the relationship with the object rejecting. But these two aspects are in contrast with each other and since the tension that arises from their conflict is threatening to the identity of the child, the latter is forced to operate in a split via a function, defined as I-reality. The concept of Fairbairn proposes the psychopathology as a result of cleavage of a primary I, unified and cohesive, but this was needed to maintain this cohesion of an object and rewarding of an environment favourable.

With the conception of the true self and the false self, Winnicott later expanded this concept. "It is not instinctual satisfaction which means that the child begins to be, to feel that life is real and worth living." (Playing and Reality). To make this happen you need a holding company that will allow him to bring a reliable source of environment that gradually emerging sense of self, which manifests itself as: feeling of being alive, integration (continuity) and customization. But if the external conditions are not favourable, the child will perceive each experience, as interference and abuse. In the face of this experience he will be forced to build a form that will become the false self, which is necessary to protect the true self from exploitation, bringing about the annihilation. But the most interesting contribution of Winnicott regards the method of object relations and processes that exist between the emerging self of the child and the external reality that surrounds him. Winnicott sought to thermalize this early interaction between child and environment, especially with the concept of potential space and intermediate area of experience, which allows him to define what is really at stake in the mental processes that enable a relationship between the subjective world and external reality. The child lives in the external world, especially the material as threatening, therefore absolutely requires an intermediary who is the mother.

Experience exchange between mother and baby can be summarized as follows: the child, instead of feeling overwhelmed by the object, can live the illusion of creating the object, but it is the mother who gives this illusion because the object was there waiting to become an object invested and creating. According to the author this creative experience creates a sense of security and confidence in the child, it was a moment of total dependence in which he is still unable to use the separation and independence. And 'the play area and the transitional object that makes it possible to separate and withdraw into themselves. "It's the only play while playing that the individual child or adult is able to be creative and to use the whole personality, and it is only in being creative that the individual discovers the self."

This discovery leads to find a way to exist as himself, to enter into a relationship with the objects, but also the ability to retreat into himself in the creative tension of these two movements the child is able to preserve their self. As there is the need to communicate there is also the need to retire and not be discovered.

"It's a joy to hide, but it is a disaster not to be found." These two authors do not directly describe narcissism, but suggest that the dynamics will be important for the understanding of this instance. A less well-known author, just in the same year, make a thorough study on narcissism: Greenberger is that in 1971, reaping the benefits of works written since 1956, publishes "The narcissism." The central thesis is as follows: narcissism is autonomous and specific psychic energy, which originates in the state of elation prenatal.

The fetus is experiencing a particular situation (eport) that is constituted by a perfect homeostasis, in the absence of needs, because these are automatically satisfied. After birth, the baby has to face the inevitable frustrations due to the relationship with reality. The persistence of this illusion will enable him to deal with the trauma of having to restructure its economy on a base object and drives. To make up for the collapse of his universe the narcissistic child needs narcissistic elements from outside. "He reads now own narcissistic confirmation in the eyes of his mother, who confirmed that it is the only and has a value." Confirmations narcissistic, from the outside, will follow the phantasy and the creation of ideals.

In healthy development, then the balance between object libido and narcissistic libido will not therefore be a balance between narcissism and object libido, but a dialectical relationship between component instinctual and narcissistic component. This theory will lead the author to consider the narcissism not only an independent factor, but also as a third force, not instinctual, which will have enormous influence on the formation of an ego healthy, effective and cohesive. Although with different arguments, assumptions Greenberger seem to be very similar to those developed independently by Kohut. According to Kohut, the self of the child requires great empathy and tenderness mirroring (mirroring) by the mother, whose presence affective ensures the consolidation of this archaic grandiose self that just on the basis of this reinforcement, gradually evolve into forms of self-esteem and self-confidence, a development that implies a less and less need for reflection.

In fact, a good relationship with the self-object will, in the course of development, the child to implement the formation of an imago (idealized self-object) and in the internalization become a stable function of the ego constitutes the ideal of 'I, that from this point on, will be the main supplier and regulator-esteem. At birth the child to maintain a sense of well-being in the face of difficulties and disappointments of external reality, creates a grandiose and exhibitionistic of the Self (grandiose Self) which is then transferred to a transitional self-object that is the mother.

And the child can maintain this positive image (grandiose Self), only if is a real object that reinforces this feeling. "The acceptance speculate mother confirms nuclear grandeur of the child, his hold and carry him allows experiences of fusion with the idealized self-object omnipotence." If you are too frustrating situations, it produces a developmental arrest and put into a grandiose Self traumatic crisis that will manifest later as narcissistic personality disorder. When these people start a dynamic psychotherapy manifest two types of transference: the idealization and the mirror.

The idealizing transference is the idealized parental imago reactivation is as if the patient said: "You are perfect and I am one of you," and therefore the patient feels empty and impotent when it is separated from the object-idealized self. The author suggests that the intensity of the dependence derives from a stop of the normal trend psychic, so balance narcissistic is only ensured by an approval and continuous attention by substitutive figures idealized self-object, lost traumatic childhood.

Transference specular highlights the reactivation of the grandiose self of the patient and can be expressed as fusion archaic transference ("You and I are one, this unit is equipped with all perfection"), twin transfer ("We two are very similar") and transfer speculate that represents a higher form of transference and which corresponds to the affirmation:

"I can see who they are in your eyes." In the case that the external inevitable frustrations are optimal, the psychic functions of the object-self and the grandiose Self will be gradually neutralized to give life to other functions, such as aspects ideals and ambitions realistic personality who will then become provider's adequate self-esteem.

"The Kohut narcissism-support-is defined not by the objective of the investment drive, but the nature and quality of cathexis." So narcissistic investment and investment object they differ in a different experiential lived. It 'clear that the narcissistic investment makes it possible to exercise control over his mind and his body, necessary possibility to overcome the weakness and dependence of the child and make him able to invest the object with safety, security and confidence that comes just from this experience. So narcissism is not only original, but it is an instance key for the development of the small man, precisely because of its intrinsic fragility and dependence. All this leads the author to suggest two lineages organization psychic lines separate but interdependent. This complex framework of development, in which the narcissism at the centre of psychic development, leads the author to define two basic types of man. The tragic man in search of himself and enjoying his creations.

Man guilty (Guilty man) who seeks pleasure in the continuous reduction of conflicts. While in a synthetic manner seems clear that the contribution of Kohut remains crucial not only for the understanding of the nature of narcissism, but also for the understanding of its distortions. As reflected in this setting that clearly suggests a genesis of structural disorder, there is Kornberg believes instead that the narcissistic pathology as a result of defensive processes archaic.

The basic defence system in the borderline syndrome, which includes the narcissistic disorder, is the cleavage, the same that, physiological in the first year of life for congenital inability integrative ego becomes, if prolonged, the mechanism psychopathological primary and original the borderline patient, in the sense that many of the characteristics of this disease are direct derivations of the split. The split is characterized by a total emotional disconnect between contradictory states of the ego, and in particular experiencing a totally split in perceptions idealized and persecutory object relations. And as long as the split persists, defuses the emergence of anxiety, the benefit that is paid with a number of serious relational problems.

A first consequence of the demerger is the dispersion of the identity, i.e. the lack of integration of opposing representations and the lack of an experienced stable of total objects in relationship with the self, with the consequent lack of integration of the Self. The most obvious manifestation of this relational identity diffusion is the division of external objects in totally good and totally bad, with the concomitant possibility of extreme fluctuations of these lived on the same object. This rapid, continuous, iterative oscillation often determines an object relational experiences of confusion and chaos. Other defence mechanisms are primitive idealization, which hides dynamic and hostile envy, denial, omnipotence and projective identification that constitutes, together with the division and dispersion of the identity of the triad pathognomonic borderline patient. Projective identification is constituted by the unconscious tendency to induce another significant attitudes or reactions due to projections of parts of the self predominantly negative and aggressive, and then check the other that is supposed to work under the dominion of these projections.

The borderline patient therefore has a rigid inner world, a loss of identity that can spill over into the disavowal of difference between self and non-self, a relational hostile and contradictory and a marked tendency to projective identification. But as it manifests the narcissistic personality disorder: I will try to make it explicit by proposing a summary of the most important AA and stressing that despite the diversity of the genetic approach, the descriptive phenomenological aspect tends to be convergent.

Typically these patients, relationships with others, they refer, with a frequency unusual in themselves, showing a great need to be loved and admired, indicating a marked contrast with the concept of hypertrophic their Self. The emotional life is characterized by the constant need to be appreciated and admired, and they feel restless, becoming irritable and aggressive when external objects that support their grandeur, they are not. There is considerable pent-up hostility and envy which leads to an idealized objects from which benefits are expected narcissistic, while devaluing and despise anyone or anything that you do not expect or do not conform to their needs and expectations.

In general the relationship with the other is based on exploitation of a more or less intense that is related to their inability to understand and identify with another. And 'as if they were convinced they had the right to control and possess others, to use them without any sense of guilt and often behind a facade sometimes brilliant and fascinating (see Fairbairn) one notices a remarkable coolness and indifference. The absence, in those subjects of any capacity for empathy, chronic anger, but often repressed, hypertrophy of the Self, the omnipotent control combined with the tendency to write-downs of the other, all often under the cover of idealization, are the false self of the narcissistic personality disorder.

If we consider the narcissism as a structure and a fundamental psychic instance to manage the dialectic of tension subject-object, which is necessary to regulate the flow of object investment and therefore also the ability to separate and recover themselves, then we can say that the alteration of this function is the narcissistic personality disorder in its expression psychopathological median.

Besides the classic narcissistic disorder, as described above, can also be structured two other events. On the one hand, the subject with a disorder of this kind may favour a tendency to hide, not to relate with each other because they are afraid of being easily frustrated. Faced with the fear of rejection that would further increase the threshold of anger and destructiveness, he prefers to withdraw and grow in this distancing one's self great. But we can also have the opposite situation: the terror of not being caught, leads the patient to a kind of reaction formation with his compulsive need to be seen, recognized, appreciated.

Their grandiose Self needs references narcissistic continue and they put in place all their ability to attract the attention and admiration of the other. In this case, personality traits, will be a megalomaniac-exhibitionistic, with inevitable cracks paranoid (persecution), when the world is not controlled, or otherwise does not exactly match the expectations of the subject. So the narcissistic disorder can have two modes of expression are very different on the phenomenal plane, much like if you look at the dynamic level. Certainly there will wonder how it is possible that from a common basic element, a single genotype (pathology of narcissism) can develop two very different phenotypes.

Psychopathology, as is evident and as we observe, is the result of a number of factors related to the individual's history, its specific moment of the life cycle, the capacity (resources) remaining undisturbed by the disease, a set relationships that may have deteriorated or influenced the disorder that is the basis of psychopathology. If we consider the complexity and interaction of these factors can be assumed that a fundamental alteration of a psychical as narcissism, can generate, but the uniqueness of the primary disorder, various phenomenal forms. So we can assume that the mental disorder instance, defined narcissism, is the basis of all personality disorders.

CHAPTER 6: CAUSE AND SYPMTOMS OF NARCISSIST PERSONALITY DISORDER

Narcissistic personality disorder — one of a few kinds of personality disorder — is a state of mind where individuals have their very own swelled feeling significance, a profound requirement for exorbitant consideration and reverence, upset connections, and an absence of sympathy for other people. Be that as it may, behind this cover of outrageous certainty lies a delicate confidence that is powerless against the smallest analysis.

A narcissistic personality disorder messes up numerous everyday disorders, for example, connections, work, school or monetary disorders. Individuals with narcissistic personality disorder might be commonly miserable and baffled when they're not given the uncommon favours or profound respect they accept they merit. They may discover their connections unfulfilling, and others may not appreciate being around them.

Treatment for narcissistic personality disorder bases on talk treatment (psychotherapy).

Manifestations

Signs and manifestations of narcissistic personality disorder and the seriousness of indications fluctuate. Individuals with the turmoil can:

- Have a misrepresented feeling of pomposity
- Have a feeling of privilege and require steady, over the top adoration
- Expect to be perceived as unrivalled even without accomplishments that warrant it
- Exaggerate accomplishments and gifts
- Be engrossed with dreams about progress, power, splendour, magnificence or the ideal mate
- Believe they are unrivalled and can just connect with similarly uncommon individuals
- Monopolize discussions and put down or look down on individuals they see as second rate

- Expect extraordinary favours and unquestioning consistence with their desires
- Take bit of leeway of others to get what they need
- Have a failure or reluctance to perceive the necessities and sentiments of others
- Be jealous of others and accept others begrudge them
- Behave in an egotistical or haughty way, appearing to be prideful, bombastic and vainglorious
- Insist on having the best of everything — for example, the best vehicle or office

Simultaneously, individuals with narcissistic personality disorder experience difficulty taking care of anything they see as analysis, and they can:

- Become restless or furious when they don't get unique treatment
- Have critical relational disorders and effectively feel insulted

- React with anger or hatred and attempt to disparage the other individual to cause themselves to seem predominant
- Have trouble controlling feelings and conduct
- Experience serious disorders managing pressure and adjusting to change
- Feel discouraged and touchy in light of the fact that they miss the mark concerning flawlessness
- Have mystery sentiments of instability, disgrace, powerlessness and embarrassment

When to see a specialist

Individuals with narcissistic personality disorder might not have any desire to believe that anything could not be right, so they might be probably not going to look for treatment. In the event that they do look for treatment, it's bound to be for manifestations of melancholy, medication or liquor use, or another emotional well-being disorder. In any case, saw put-down to confidence may make it hard to acknowledge and finish treatment.

On the off chance that you perceive parts of your personality that are regular to narcissistic personality disorder or you're feeling overpowered by bitterness, consider connecting with a confided in specialist or emotional well-being supplier. Getting the correct treatment can help make your life all the more fulfilling and agreeable.

Solicitation an Appointment at Mayo Clinic

Causes

It's not recognized what causes narcissistic personality disorder. Likewise with personality improvement and with other psychological well-being disorder, the reason for narcissistic personality disorder is likely intricate. Narcissistic personality disorder might be connected to:

- Environment — confuses in parent-youngster associations with either exorbitant veneration or unnecessary analysis that is inadequately receptive to the kid's understanding

- Genetics — acquired qualities
- Neurobiology — the association between the cerebrum and conduct and thinking

Hazard factors

Narcissistic personality disorder influences a bigger number of guys than females, and it regularly starts in the adolescents or early adulthood. Remember that, albeit a few youngsters may show attributes of narcissism, this may essentially be common of their age and doesn't mean they'll proceed to create narcissistic personality disorder.

Despite the fact that the reason for narcissistic personality disorder isn't known, a few analysts imagine that in naturally defenceless kids, child parenting styles that are overprotective or careless may have an effect. Hereditary qualities and neurobiology additionally may assume a job being developed of narcissistic personality disorder.

Entanglements

Entanglements of narcissistic personality disorder, and different conditions that can happen alongside it, can include:

- Relationship challenges
- Problems at work or school
- Depression and uneasiness
- Physical medical disorders
- Drug or liquor abuse
- Suicidal considerations or conduct

Avoidance

Since the reason for narcissistic personality disorder is obscure, there's no realized method to forestall the condition. Be that as it may, it might help to:

- Get treatment at the earliest opportunity for youth psychological wellness disorders
- Participate in family treatment to learn sound approaches to convey or to adapt to clashes or passionate misery
- Attend child parenting classes and look for direction from advisors or social labourers if necessary

CHAPTER 7 - WHEN TENDENCIES STICK IN NPD

Take this for instance:

George had just about had enough of his father's behavior. He didn't like being belittled, torn down, and compared to his dad, and he hated having his hard work underappreciated simply because he was 'just his father's son.' So, after their last heated argument, he decided to just walk away and leave their relationship at that. Whether they'd ever been on good terms again, he was uncertain. But he was happy to finally be free from his dad's abuse.

In the weeks following his falling out with his dad, George started to feel a strong sense of isolation and guilt. He felt as though he had wronged his father, and struggled to resist the urge to reconcile, knowing full well that it would only give his dad the fuel he needed to make George feel bad about protecting and defending himself.

George would soon start to realize all the little narcissistic behaviors that his father manifested throughout his childhood up until his adulthood. He realized that all the expensive family vacations his father would splurge on weren't for their enjoyment, but to show others around them that he had the financial capabilities to pay for such expensive outings.-

He noticed that as he and his siblings were growing up, their father would always pick a favorite who he would praise and validate to the point where all the other siblings felt like they had to compete to get the same treatment. He realized that his father rarely had anything good to say about anyone, and that he particularly seemed to enjoy talking harsh negativities about everyone around him.

By thinking about his father's behavior, George soon discovered that he had been acting similarly. He noticed how he would also be critical of others, how he often thought he was better than many of his coworkers, and how he found it tough to deal with criticism from others. In a lot of ways, he had assimilated his father's behavior and was showing borderline narcissistic tendencies in many of his interactions.

Needless to say, staying too long with a narcissist can make this a possibility.

Especially for children of narcissists, assimilating narcissistic behavior is a very real danger. However, a sudden severance of a relationship with a narcissist, especially if it happens in a confrontational way, can help the abused snap out of the spell and see the narcissistic tendencies in themselves.

So, if you've just left an abusive relationship with a narcissist who made up a large part of your life, you might start to notice that you've started to adopt some of the behaviors they've shown you. Often, it's the sense of inflated self-esteem and the critical view of others that sticks around more noticeably.

Upon realizing this, you might feel worried thinking that there's no way to turn back. After all, narcissists can't change. So, what does the future look like for you? Remember that narcissistic people struggle to change because of their outlook. They can't recognize that they're doing anything wrong, so they don't feel the need to fix anything.

However, since you've already noticed that there's an error in the way that you operate in social situations, it will become much more possible and viable for you to make a change in your life.

HOW TO ERASE THE NARC'S EFFECTS

You already know how it felt to be abused by a narcissist, and it's likely that you won't want to inflict the same damage on the people around you. Some people who were subjected to narcissistic abuse claim to want to erase the narc's effects because they want to distance themselves from their abuser completely, not wanting any of their residue in their lives.

Whatever the case might be with you, it's very possible to erase narcissistic tendencies once you become aware of them. Following these steps should help set you off in the right direction towards becoming a better person.

BE MINDFUL

In a lot of ways, the effects of the narcissist might be moderately to severely ingrain in your psyche as well. Of course, this might change depending on how close you were with your abuser, and how much power they truly had over your life. In many cases, the most severe effects exist in the children of narcissists since parents are often the biggest influence in our lives.

Now that you know the kind of effect your abuser had, it's ideal that you maintain mindfulness since many of the behaviors you've learned are likely reflexive. What does that mean? Simply put, you might find that the tendencies you've adapted are not actually things that you still have to think about in order to manifest. They show up even when you're not trying, making you act in ways that you otherwise would try to avoid.

Maintaining mindfulness on the different ways that you might show narcissism isn't easy. Despite that, it is possible to train your mind so that you learn to undo the behavior. This involves becoming more tactful and thinking more deliberately before you act or speak.

Right before you make a move, try to ask yourself these questions:

Am I acting out of a sense of self-entitlement?

Will anything good come out of my words/actions?

Am I doing this to cause insult to others, or to make them feel inferior to me?

Do I have a valid reason to dislike this person and to act out on my feelings?

Although you might take some time thinking about the repercussions and the motives behind your thoughts, going through this process of weighing your actions before you execute them can help you avoid acting out like your abuser.

Over time, the process will become instinctual, allowing you to erase the tendencies all together.

LEARN TO ACCEPT OTHERS' ADVANTAGES

One of the things that narcissistic victims tend to admit is that they have the tendency to look down on other people and their achievements. This is the result of the narcissist initially treating you like an extension of him or herself.

They only want to associate themselves with people who deserve to be in their presence, so it's possible that you might have heard them tell you how smart, beautiful, talented, gifted, or capable you are. With time, this can make you think that you are better than the others around you, just like your narcissistic abuser.

The 'us versus them' mentality is a popular tactic used by narcissists to strengthen their victims' feelings of oneness. The more you feel united with your abuser, the more likely you'll submit to their demands and expectations.

Now that you've severed the ties, you might start to notice how you have the tendency to look down on others and think of yourself as the better person in most social situations. You might see how you tend to dislike it when other people do better than you, and you resort to nitpicking to find something that they're bad at to make yourself feel better.

In these instances, it's important to remind yourself that different people have different strengths, and you can't be the best at everything. There will always be others who are better than you at certain activities or tasks, and that's not a problem. That doesn't mean that you amount to less, you don't need to feel threatened by other people's success.

ERASE THE AGGRESSION

Being around a narcissist might have made it reflexive for you to look at most social interactions as though they're confrontational and aggressive in nature, even if the people you encounter aren't trying to spark an argument. This is often the result of the narcissist telling you're better than other people, a necessary aspect of establishing the 'us versus them' mentality.

Now, when you're in a social situation, your initial tendency might be to act dominating and aggressive, asserting yourself even when it isn't necessary just to reinforce your abuser's idea that you're better than the others you encounter.

Try to adapt a more neutral response to social interactions and react based on what you're shown instead of being confrontational off the bat.

It's entirely possible to develop narcissistic traits despite being abused in the relationship. Remember, the narcissist's tactics involve making you feel like you're on the same level, which may cause you to develop a sense of importance, entitlement, and inflated self-worth.

Recognizing where these behaviors might manifest themselves, developing your mindfulness, and working to improve yourself as you continue the process of healing can help you escape the trend to become much less like your abuser, and more of a well-rounded, level-headed individual.

CHAPTER 8 - COPING WITH OUTSIDERS LOOKING IN NPD

A common issue that victims of narcissistic abuse have to deal with but don't often expect is the pressure of explaining themselves to the people in their circle.

That's the problem with being in any sort of relationship with a narcissist; connections are rarely ever private. So, there are going to be a lot of people who might be wondering why you're suddenly no longer seen together.

To the healing victim, these questions might seem like the ideal opportunity to open up and talk about the abuse that they'd been through. But it often proves to be a pitfall because many of those around you might still see the narcissist in a positive light.

THE STRUGGLE OF ISOLATION

In many ways, the healing can feel like treading a lonely road. It's rare that you'll have someone from your family and friends who can truly understand what you're going through. If they're close with the abuser, they may even act in favor of the narcissist and inflict more pain and hurt on you.

Throughout this process, you need to understand that having someone there to help you through the healing might be impossible unless you're able to find a support group to help you out. That's why it's always best to help yourself and seek out support if you feel that it's necessary for your emotional and mental health and wellbeing.

Why do people abandon the victim of narcissistic abuse? Simple: the narcissist might have already beaten you to the punch line. Knowing that you've disengaged from the relationship, your abuser already has an idea that you likely have a few bad things to say about them. Since they're intensely invested in their image, they do their best to make sure that none of that information makes its way into the mainstream. So, the moment you walked away, it's likely that the narcissist had already painted a picture of you to your common friends and family. Ultimately, their objective was to make sure that you had as little credibility as possible, so anything you might say later would have little likelihood of being believed.

In some cases, a narcissist might even encourage others to avoid you all together. They do this by inflating your mistakes, making you look like a severely bad person, and telling others to 'watch out' because you might do the same thing to them.

The reason why this works, even if you've been nothing but friendly, helpful, and honest with the people around you, is because a narcissist will always have a much more polished image than you do. They're seen as ideal individuals, and the idea that you might have crossed them comes across as unreasonable. What reason would you have to be so upset with someone who's so well-rounded?

ALL THE WRONG REASONS

If you're lucky enough to have family and friends that are strangers to your abuser, then you might be able to vent and talk about your situation in a less critical space. However, it's important to understand that just because they don't know your abuser, doesn't mean they'll be able to provide reasonable, actionable advice.

For instance, Tracy, who had finally decided to leave her abusive, narcissistic husband after suffering through poor treatment for nearly 10 years, comes to her close workmate and best friend who hasn't met or seen her husband. Tracy opens up about the difficulties, the control, and the emotional and mental manipulation that has her broken, beaten, and close to depressed.

Of course, her friend sympathizes with her and tells her that everything will be fine. But a main theme in her advice is that Tracy should give her husband another chance. "He's your husband after all. Do you really want to sacrifice your marriage for an attitude problem? There are people who have seen worse but still manage to soldier through. Maybe he's going through a phase."

The reason why the others around you might find it easy to say things like this is because they've never dealt with a narcissist before. It is true, relationships formed through binding covenants such as marriage, can be harder to toss out the window because of the promises you've made. But harmonious coexistence with a narcissist is rarely achievable.

Others can easily try to cope with the bad habits and attitudes of their close friends and family and say that it's an effort borne of love. But if you're dealing with a narcissist, love is hardly a sound solution. These people can't interpret affection and love, and only see positive reception of their being as praise and admiration. So, any love that you might offer will be seen as submissiveness and acknowledgment of their superiority.

Hearing other people in your circle telling you to be more patient, to extend yourself, to consider the role the abuser has played in your life can make you second-guess your decision to walk away. But keep in mind that these people are speaking from a completely different vantage point and likely have no experience dealing with a narcissist at all.

While it's alright to vent and seek support from friends and family that have no ties with your abuser, it's always best to consider where they're coming from when they decide to impart any sort of advice. People who have no experience with narcissists might give you recommendations that don't really fit your situation, so take it in stride and be secure in your decision to leave. No one knows what's better for you other than yourself.

The road to recovery can be a long and lonely one. Often, you will have difficulty finding a support group that can actually relate to and understand your situation. That's because narcissists are exceptionally gifted at hiding their truth, so most people won't know the real nature of your abuser even if you exhaust yourself trying to explain it. What's more, not all people have encounters with narcissists, so the odds of finding someone who can fully understand your situation can be a challenge.

But don't lose hope. These days, it's possible to find support groups for narcissistic abuse victims, allowing you access to a variety of resources, stories, and companionship that can help you soldier through the healing process with the right guidance and reassurance.

CHAPTER 9: INTERPERSONAL RELATIONS IN NARCISSIST DISORDER

The person with Narcissistic Personality Disorder shows typical, continuous and pervasive features person logical as exaggerated sense superiority, megalomania and perennial need for admiration. Therefore the personality revolves around excessive feelings of grandiosity and uniqueness, with the consideration to be special and above any other individual. The behaviours are frequently arrogant, proud and full of snobbish and disdainful attitudes. For this reason he is very sensitive to even the smallest and inconsistent statements or criticism, and / or any possible setbacks or failures in various functional areas of life (emotional, social, work, family, etc.).

These personality traits, focusing on exaggerated account of themselves, involve attitudes of excessive anger, strong discouragement, and stress, intense depression towards dynamic bankruptcy and / or ideas and critical words from people more or less close. Sometimes by exaggerating judgment on their own behalf the individual with Narcissistic Personality is taken from imaginative ideas have personal and unlimited success, power, beauty, etc.. Approaching their story and picture to that of people who are already very popular, preferred and success. The individual with Narcissistic Personality Disorder believes to be superior and / or special, expecting others to recognize such a thing. This belief leads to more convictions of attending or feel understood only by other special people and / or high social status.

The socio-emotional individual with Narcissistic Personality are then also influenced so dysfunctional excess of ego, the constant demands for attention and admiration and claims need to fulfil as soon as possible (again based on the presumed superiority). In this way there is the belief and conviction that it is normal to use and exploit others with respect to their needs, which are considered much more important and special than others, it is then justified the insistence of care and treatments. There is a continuing need for compliments and praise, with the worry of when and in what quantity uploads the admiration and the envy of other people, not by chance that no consideration is taken with awe and / or aggression and dysphonic mood. It 'also this fact, the conviction of being envied and / or envy towards the same things and successes of others, collected and written down as undeserved and a source of resentment and angry attitude. Who is present in the Narcissistic Personality Disorder is, in other words, the perennial expectation of having to be seen and met, and when it does not generate confusion and anger.

The person is therefore expected that the date is given and whatever he wants (e.g. dedication), going beyond any legitimate right space and the needs of others. Often another feature is the strong ambition which may involve good school results and working, but still hides the superficiality and fragility of relationships relational and affective, with little or no empathy. Sometimes, however, the performance work or school can be very low, pointing to the obvious personal aversion to accept any failures, risks and critical in certain competitive situations or other in which it is possible to note a bitter defeat. And 'in fact present, as mentioned, selfishness, exploitation, manipulation towards others, where the widespread sense of entitlement and lack of sensitivity to the desires and needs of others, can result in the exploitation of other voluntary or involuntary.

As described is also evident in a large fragile self-esteem, enthralled by the constant need for approval and attention, as well as the ever-present expectation of special treatment, admiration and praise, and no tolerance for criticism also very small. Self-esteem is enhanced when an individual voluntarily with Narcissistic Personality reflects the, so to speak, in the idealization of the supposed high values and characteristics of people who are busy. Thus, there is the insistence to have contact only with those deemed "better." In addition, he tends to create relationships, friendships or relationships sentimental type only if it appears possible that the other person can help some of his intentions and can satisfy all the personality traits described above. Interpersonal relations are then compromised precisely because of the problems caused by repeated claims, demands of praise and admiration, and lack of interest in psycho-emotional feelings and needs of others. Individuals with Narcissistic Personality Disorder show a general emotional coldness and are also deficient in empathy and emotional intelligence, or have great difficulty in recognizing desires, needs, feelings and problems of other people, and when they are approved shall be seen as signs of weakness or vulnerability.

In summary in the individual with Narcissistic Personality Disorder is found a picture person logical highlighted by grandiosity with overestimation of their real capacity (due to the devaluation and underestimate those of others), exaggeration with respect to their true virtue and knowledge, need for admiration and attention, lack of empathy and excessive presumption and arrogance. The self-esteem of the individual with Narcissistic Personality Disorder, being very sensitive to the so-called "narcissistic injuries" due to criticism, is very vulnerable. In this way also the mood can flex so problematic generating additional Mood Disorders (e.g. Depression or Dysthymia), and can occur gradually and dysfunctional social withdrawal and affective relationship with the possible appearance of Anxiety Disorders.

Based on the typical traits of Narcissistic Personality may also occur over extended periods of excessive grandeur and activities, alternating with periods of intense deactivation and depressed mood, or a bipolar disorder, as well as Eating Disorders (e.g. anorexia) or Related Disorders Substance- with abuse and / or dependence on one or more substances (e.g. cocaine). Finally, the Narcissistic Personality Disorder may also be associated with other disorders such as Antisocial Personality, Borderline, Histrionic and / or Paranoid. The pathological liars are people disturbed and disturbing that in order to implement the necessary fiction they declare themselves supporters of absolute sincerity and its values.

This is sick, even if they appear normal on the surface, and their disorder can cause serious consequences to those around them. Are people with narcissistic personality disorder which are not fully aware of their disease and believe that it is right to lie in order to protect your ego and realize the benefits, to the point of serious damage to others with ruthlessly manipulative behaviour? In the scale of psychiatric disorders narcissists are liars-just before the psychopaths or serial killers, or at least those people who are disturbed that in addition to lie and to practice moral violence without mercy, even commit acts of extreme physical cruelty. The narcissistic pathological liars do not come to this, but with their moral violence steeped in attitudes and behaviour that is misleading, they can - without being the slightest scruple - generate enormous suffering to their victims and in some cases can reach inciting suicide. It is a serious disorder that is creeping for many years and then explodes at the level blown leading to tragic unhappiness on the relational and existential (loneliness and anxiety) and various psychological disorders (then incurable), even in different forms of splitting personality (schizophrenia).

Individuals who have a narcissistic personality disorder show a significant impairment in work, social and emotional. The vulnerability of self-esteem makes them remarkably sensitive to negative judgments: Although often cannot show it outwardly, in fact, tend to experience them as real humiliation for their source of deep dejection and despair. From a relational point of view can sometimes react to criticism with anger and rage, fighting back with insolence, and sometimes the experience can lead to avoidance of disapproval or social withdrawal, starting by feelings of inadequacy and shame. If reciprocate a favour or respond to a moral obligation, are generally compelled to do so to receive admiration, rather than for reasons of respect to the recipient of their act. From a business point of view, though the high ambition can lead to important results such individuals, intolerance to criticism tends to seriously affect their performance.

In this sense, the operation professional or, more generally, the performance in the performance of various nature, can be rather modest, due to the reluctance of such individuals to accept the risk in situations in which it is possible to a failure or a defeat or must negotiate their goals with colleagues. Finally, from an emotional point of view, the excessive demand for admiration, together with the assumption of arrogant attitudes on the one hand, careless and detached the other hand, greatly affect the quality of relationships established. In general, the area of emotional relationships is compromised in this disorder: relationships are unpleasant for the person himself and this can cause intense suffering for the partner.

In an essay of 1931, "Types lewd", Sigmund Freud described the narcissistic personality. The characteristics of the third type, justly called the narcissistic, are in their negatively described. There is tension between ego and superego - in fact, starting from this type would hardly have arrived at the concept of superego, there is no preponderance of erotic needs, the main interest is focused on self-preservation, and the type is independent and not easily intimidated. The ego has at its disposal a considerable amount of aggression, one manifestation of this is the propensity activity, where love is concerned, and love is preferred to being loved. People of this type impress others as being 'personalities', it is on them that their peers are likely to lean, they readily assume the role of leader, give a fresh stimulus to cultural development or breakdown existing conditions.

Wilhelm Reich first described the "phallic-narcissistic personality" in 1926, and later included the description in 'Personality Analysis. Even in outward appearance, the phallic-narcissistic personality differs from compulsive and hysterical. While the compulsive personality is predominantly inhibited, self-controlled and depression, and while the hysterical personality is nervous, agile, nervous and unstable, the typical phallic-narcissistic self-confident, often arrogant, elastic, vigorous and often impressive. The more neurotic the inner mechanism, more obtrusive are those patterns of behaviour. As physical, they belong more frequently to

Kretschmer's athletic type. The facial expression typically appears tough, masculine features, but often female, girl-like features, in spite of athletic habitus. The behaviour of every day is never crawling as in passive-feminine personality's, but usually haughty, either cold and reserved or derisively aggressive, or "shaggy", as he called one of these patients.

Behaviour towards the object, including the object of love, the narcissistic element always dominates object-libidinal, and there is always a mixture of sadistic traits more or less disguised. These individuals usually anticipate any attack with an attack of their own. Their aggression is often expressed not so much in what they say or do, but as they say and do things. In particular, they appear as aggressive and provocative to people who do not have their own aggression at their disposal.

The outspoken types tend to achieve leading positions in life and resent subordination unless they can - as in the army or in hierarchical organizations

- Compensate for the necessity of subordination by exerting control over others who are in the lower rungs of the ladder. If their vanity is hurt, or react with cold reserve to deep depression or lively aggression.

In contrast to the other personalities, their narcissism is expressed not in a childlike way, but in a demonstration of exaggerated self-confidence, dignity and superiority, despite the fact that the basis of their personality is no less childish than the other. In a chapter of Disorders of narcissism: diagnostic implications, clinical and experimental, "DSM Narcissistic Personality Disorder historical reflections and future directions", Theodore Million, differs from narcissistic personality disorder narcissistic compensatory. Reich (1933/1949) has captured the essential qualities of what is here called the elitist narcissistic person when he described the personality "phallic narcissistic" as a person self-confident, arrogant and energetic "often impressive in his bearing and ill-suited to positions subordinate in the hierarchy ". As regards the person narcissistic compensatory, the elitist narcissistic person is more taken from an image of the inflated self from its real self. Both narcissistic types create a facade that bears minimal resemblance to the real person.

However, the compensatory narcissistic person knows at some level be a cheat in fact, where the elitist narcissistic person is deeply convinced of his self-image above, although based on a few realistic results. For people narcissistic elitist is the appearance of what is perceived as objective reality, inflated self-image is their intrinsic substance.

Only when these illusory elements of self-worth are seriously called into question the individual will be able to recognize, and perhaps even take note of his deepest flaws.

We live in a society "narcissistic" where beauty, emotional distance from intimate relationships, perfection and happiness pseudo encase us in a way of living life artefact. It seems that no one is immune from narcissistic personality disorder, each of us has our own dose of narcissism to which clings stubbornly proud: it is difficult, therefore, be able to distinguish a narcissism in a well-integrated personality from a narcissistic personality disorder.

However, there are alarm bells that are usually detectable in the quality of relationships that a person with narcissistic personality disorder tends to establish. Who is suffering from a narcissistic personality disorder has a deep pain so powerful that lead to a kind of anaesthesia to all that is emotion, sentiment and love. His inability to love comes out especially in the affective relationship: it is incapable of empathy, caring and is unable to take care of others, does not feel real concern for the other, cannot sustain long ties and, overwhelmed by the versatility of its behaviours artefacts tend to end relationships on relationships. The partner is functional, often, only to meet their own needs: the other becomes the object, not of love, interchangeably as a Kleenex, unable to relate to anything, not only does not provide that the partner may have of the needs that exist apart from him, but as soon as it advances the requests, it is immediately replaced and left. In addition, people suffering from narcissistic personality disorder is unable to experience pleasure, boredom, apathy and depression and dysthymic lived are always lurking.

The Narcissistic Personality Disorder, or rather, narcissism, implies the tendency of the individual to constantly invest energy efficiency of the self to itself. What you create is an energy circuit closed and pathology lies the exchange energy, which means emotional, affective and relational between himself and the world: the narcissist is always set up position with respect to another saying used and placed in a down position. All this serves to narcissistic to consistently meet their ego ideal: to hear one thing and be another, loneliness and lack of contact, claims, first of all, to themselves, to be unique and special, accompany life the narcissist. Narcissism, like all diseases and symptoms are a clever attempt to adapt to life, to a intrauterine environment and family where you are made experiences that are alarming, castrating, frustrating, supported by a superego parental narcissistic project that later became falsely your own.

Narcissism thus becomes the golden cage in which the child becomes an adult, the way hyper-trophic clings to life, replacing it is capable of loving a constant effort to maintain a high ego ideal, touching, whenever that this ideal is threatened, the risk of depressive and dysthymic, thus reviving the alarm and frustration of that child, now an adult, not accepted in an authentic way. In this view, narcissism is a position, not a personality trait, which, like the sadism and masochism may develop to varying degrees throughout the life span, parallel to the evolutionary phases and their respective incisions which help to structure personality, and the armour of the individual.

It is not surprising that narcissism is associated with a range of interpersonal problems. The narcissist induces another a positive first impression that, in the long run, gives way to negative feelings. On the other hand, in romantic relationships, these people tend to partners who can keep up their self-esteem, scrambling over to meet their every order. As a result, they are often not very empathetic, very critic, hostile and aggressive towards those who tend to act as a barrier to their emergence. Despite these negative interpersonal, there are also substantial positive aspects. For example, narcissists who exhibit high levels of self-esteem have lower levels of depression, anxiety and loneliness.

They also tend to report more happiness and subjective well-being than those who are less daffodils. Despite this apparent blanket of iron, narcissists are very fragile and have a high sense of inferiority and worthlessness. To cope with these feelings of inferiority, narcissists use defence strategies against those who act as threat, real or perceived, to self-esteem. This constant battle with external provocations, leads these people to implement the defensive and repressive coping strategies, which leads to increased cardiovascular reactivity, high stress, high blood pressure, and worse outcomes in cardiovascular disease, of which the Narcissists are not at all aware of it. Given that narcissism is associated with defensive strategies, and the defence has physiological consequences, it follows that narcissists can be highly reactive physical systems, and this can lead to chronic hyper-activation of the physiological system in response to stress, which in the long term could weaken the body's natural defences.

The cardiovascular reactivity associated with maintaining a positive view of themselves, active, consequently, the hypothalamic-pituitary-adrenal axis, with relative secretion of cortisol. A recent study shows that men with high scores on narcissism, have greater increases in cortisol after stressful situations, which does not occur in those who have narcissistic traits. In addition, men have a higher basal concentration of cortisol than women. Thus, it is possible that narcissist's males have a greater cardiovascular reactivity, with obvious consequences for their health. These data were not confirmed on narcissists Females, in which the chronic activation of cortisol can lead to different problems, such as suppression of the functioning of the immune system.

Maybe it's because women have a different role in society than men, who somehow have to prove their social dominance, confirming the theory of narcissism. Perhaps the female narcissists use their role for personal gain, in order to achieve social and financial resources indirectly. The hypothesis to be tested, in order to understand why the narcissism seems to be more harmful to men than women. According to Kornberg is within this type of organization personality that fit all of Personality Disorders, including Narcissistic divided into three different types.

- The healthy narcissism which we all share, in which the libidinal investment of an integrated self leads to be ambitious, to have interpersonal relationships and be consistent with your values.

- In the infantile narcissism, based on the gratification / satisfaction of needs, including the need to enter into connection with each other, the subject, as a child, is insatiably applicant, incessantly demanding and others exist only in relation to the satisfaction of his needs.

- Finally, pathological narcissism, which is configured as a specific personality disorder, arises from a hyper-libido on him. A self is not integrated, which keeps split idealized representations of self and other, thus giving rise to a grandiose self.

According to Kornberg the narcissistic patient apparently seems to work well because at first glance, the behaviour might appear little disturbed. However, investigating deeper we find that I, composed only of idealized aspects of the Self and the Object (the other), it has become "great." Thus the narcissistic patient moves in a dangerous reality, because at every moment the image grandiose that has of itself can be invalidated. To grope to defend against this risk, the narcissist is forced to keep out others who automatically become the subject of anger and devaluation.

This sharp devaluation of the other, but not enough to put away the negative emotions. Unfortunately, in fact, the narcissist must also deal with extreme feelings of inferiority generated by a sadistic superego, that trigger is an excessive need to be reassured that a deep feeling of envy towards others. The other is that it is a saviour who loved a hated rival. The relationship with other frequently becomes parasitic and based on the exploitation for food self-esteem. All of these experiences are inscribed in a deep sense of loneliness, which Kornberg called magnificent loneliness in which they are immersed these patients.

The most dramatic development of the disorder is observed when the patient's grandiosity is combined with a high proportion of aggression. In this process, the "malignant narcissism." This particular form of narcissism leads the patient to add to his grandiose self a component of omnipotence "I can do whatever I want. For me, the rules do not apply. "In this category are patients whose grandeur is enhanced by the sense of triumph tried inflicting pain and fear to others. Currently there is an indiscriminate use of the term: it speaks of narcissistic defences, narcissistic wounds, phallic narcissism, narcissistic trauma, narcissistic personality disorder, which makes it lose any specificity, until, in clinical use, to reduce this complexity to simplistic diction of healthy or pathological narcissism: this tells us little about the real situation psychopathology of the subject, but still cheaper than the real nature of narcissism.

Narcissists love themselves too much to be able to love others. For the "narcissus", love is a game where doing the "lion's share", which keep the power even if it means lying, betraying and humiliating your partner. Do not confuse narcissism with self-esteem because self-esteem fits well with the ability to love, narcissism necessarily involves the exploitation and humiliation of the partner. Of course, often narcissists are extremely attractive, but the test of the heart, gradually reveal their true nature: selfish, unfaithful, manipulative, arrogant, hypocritical ("hypocrite" in ancient Greece meant actor) The manipulator is a kind of relational pathological personality narcissistic, egocentric, a psycho-emotional vampire that feeds on the vital essence of its prey. Criticism, contempt, blame, blackmail, reminding other moral principles or the pursuit of perfection, but only when useful.

And to achieve its goals resorts to deception, pseudo-logical reasoning tipping situations to his own advantage. Often his communication is paradoxical messages opposites in double bind, which is impossible to answer without contradicting itself, or distorts the meaning of the speech. Self-commiserating, it removes responsibility, not make demands explicit and clear. Yet it does not tolerate waste, it always has the last word to draw his own conclusions, while not shared. Dumb opinions and decisions. Especially mind, suggests suspects, reports misunderstandings. Simulates somatic and self-devaluation, but it shows basically emotional neglect. That's why they are disturbed and disturbing personality: they are destabilizing and binding to them is destabilized.

CHAPTER 10: FROM NARCISSIST MYTH TO PHENOMENOLOGY

Pathological narcissism is a personality disorder more common in these times. The origins of the theme can be traced in classical literature, in Greek mythology, in fact, this is the narration of the story of Narcissus, the son of Cephissus, river god and the nymph Liriope.

According to the myth told by Ovid in his "Metamorphoses" Narcissus was a beautiful youth, all of which, both women and men, fell in love madly. However Narcissus preferred to spend his days hunting, oblivious of his admirers, among them was the nymph Echo, who was sentenced to Juno to repeat the last words that were addressed, because his talk distracted the goddess, preventing discover the loves of furtive Jupiter. Narcissus rejected by the nymph, consumed by love, he hid in the woods until they disappear and remain only a distant echo. Not only Eco, but all the young and the young despised by Narcissus, invoked the vengeance of the gods. Narcissus was sentenced by Nemesis, to fall in love with his own reflection in the water. Desperate because he could not satisfy the passion he felt, was consumed in useless lamentation, repeated by Eco. Realizing the impossibility of his love, Narcissus let himself die.

When the naiads and dryads tried his body to be able to be placed on the funeral pyre, found near the body of water the flower of the same name. It is said that Narcissus, when he crossed the Styx, the river of the dead, to enter the Underworld, looked out on the river, always hoping to see themselves reflected. But he could not see anything because of the nature murky, muddy those waters. In the end, however, Narcissus was happy not to see his reflection because this would mean that the child himself-he loved, he was not dead yet. In Boeotia version of the young Narcissus, Tepsi citizen, was sentenced to love his image, when Armenia, a local young man, he contemptuously refused, took his own life in front of his house, with the same sword that Narcissus had sent as macabre invitation not to give him more boredom.

The myth of Narcissus also lives in the play of the playwright and poet William Shakespeare (15641616), through the personality of Malvolio, who is observing the public as clearly suffering from an excessive love for himself associated with the tendency to take minor offenses for devastating attacks.

Going from the narration of myth to explain the phenomenology of narcissism is to say, first, that the difference between the levels of healthy narcissism and pathological narcissism is very difficult to grasp. A certain amount of self-love, esteem and self-respect, is not only normal but desirable but in each individual. It is not easy to identify the point along an imaginary continuum of self, where the healthy narcissism is transformed into pathological narcissism. Certainly the criterion of the evaluation phase of the life cycle through which an individual, is a useful indicator, just think, for example, the assessment benign one feels towards a teenage boy, who spends an hour every morning in the mirror before out to make perfect every hair of his hairstyle.

On the contrary, the opinion is not favourable arouse a man thirty years engaged in the same task, perhaps too much to that age do, and finally, again empathy and a sense of understanding that would result from observing a 45 year old man, struggling with the mid-life crisis, which is also absorbed long before the mirror to find the hairstyle for him nicer. Even the consideration and respect of cultural differences in which an individual is immersed, may help to assess if the dose of narcissism is healthy when, in fact, excessive. Certainly the contemporary Western society has adopted a narcissistic culture, where the media lead to appropriate the values of aesthetics, image, to appear at the expense of being, the depth and substance of things and where fear of aging and death are removed and denied. If, then, the evolutionary differences and cultural influences are valid indicators, however, forms healthy or pathological Narcissus, however, are mainly identified by considering the quality of object relations of the subject.

In fact, within the sphere of interpersonal relationships, a constant that characterizes the individual suffering from pathological narcissism is suffering, emptiness and loneliness associated with the inability to love. On the one hand, interpersonal relationships of healthy narcissistic, we can identify some key features such as empathy and concern for the feelings of others, genuine interest in the ideas of others, ability to tolerate ambivalence in long-term relationships rather than achieving a break and recognize their contribution in interpersonal conflicts.

On the other hand, in the interpersonal relations of the pathological narcissist is found that: approaches to treating others as objects to use and leave according to the narcissistic needs, regardless of their feelings, who does not live like other people who have a life separate or unique needs, often interrupts a report after a short period of time, when the partner starts making demands on their needs. In the psychological literature, many authors have dealt with the description of the various aspects of the continuum between healthy and pathological narcissism. Among them, names such as Kohut, who described the type of hyper-vigilant narcissist: a type or vulnerable, prone to fragmentation of self, highly sensitive to the reactions of others, inhibited, shy or even lead to slip away and avoid being the centre of attention and Kornberg, who described the type of narcissist unconsciously, a type envious, greedy, that requires attention and acclaim from others, not aware of the reactions of others, arrogant and aggressive, "transmitter", but not "receiving". Although these types can occur in pure form, many individuals show a mixture of phenomenological characteristics of both types.

CHAPTER 11: BEHAVIOR IN NARCISSIST & NARCISSIM PERSONALITY DISORDER

Individuals with NPD have a grandiose sense of self. They routinely overestimate their abilities, inflate their results appear boastful, arrogant and pretentious. This belief in personal superiority is the "bedrock" of their self-image. Individuals with NPD believe that their presumption of superiority is a sufficient proof of its existence. They are able to feel safe and satisfied if they think highly of themselves. The negative aspects of the self are met with denial or rationalization. However, to maintain the belief that they are superior, often without achievements, can create a painful disparity between their competence authentic and the illusory.

The effort to maintain a positive false can lead to feelings of fraudulence, emptiness and feelings of hopelessness. Individuals with NPD have a sense of their psychological fragility. They can experience a grandiose self-or a depleted, shamed. With external affirmation can feel self-righteous, arrogant, contemptuous of others, self-sufficient, and vain. With the loss of external validation, may feel a vague sense of falseness, envy, ugliness and inferiority. They seem to have little awareness that their behaviour may be considered objectionable or irrational.

People with NPD expect that others will submerge their wants for the solace and welfare of people with NPD. They accept that since they need something - that is a purpose behind it. They expect that others are devoured by worry for individuals with NPD as the people themselves, they accept they merit uncommon thought from others (DSM IV ™, 1994,). Narcissistic people use others to satisfy their own mental needs and to keep up the solidness of oneself, others are esteemed as they give comfort and enthusiastic dependability. People with NPD experience difficulty helping out others as their emphasis is on themselves.

Others consider it to be vassals or constituents; look for appreciation to their own vainglory and to keep up their top position.

They experience issues perceiving the experience and sentiments of others. They need sympathy and structure hardly any certified enthusiastic responsibilities. They should, consistently, be appreciated. On the off chance that you can perceive the necessities of others, they will in general consider these to be as indications of shortcoming and powerlessness (DSM-IV ™, 1994). People with NPD are frequently jealous of others and accept that others are desirous of them. Resent others for the things they claim and for their accomplishments. They believe they're essential to the point that others ought to concede to them, and their feeling of qualification is obvious in their absence of affectability and self-important misuse of others (DSM-IV ™, 1994). NPD confidence is delicate and kept up by outside. These people are engrossed by how they are seen by others. They improve their mental self-view by partner with individuals who are likewise prevalent, extraordinary or exceptional and of high status, they need to be in association with individuals similarly glorified worth.

The reports of those with NPD are undermined for the feeling of privilege, requirement for reverence, and absence of respect for the sentiments of others. People with NPD are relationally exploitative, they anticipate extraordinary favours without corresponding duties. Their capacity to feel love for others is minor and have just the sort of sympathy that permits them to control and adoration from others. Can be socially effortless, lovely and charming; be that as it may, can't react with genuine sympathy and can be contemptuous and unreliable. Their relationship must have a potential for propelling their objectives and upgrade their confidence. With no obvious, a relationship has no reason and is probably not going to be supported.

A grave concern in regards to people with serious NPD is cold enchantment and wantonness, their powerlessness to remain in affection, and their failure to genuinely comprehend or acknowledge the interbreeding forbidden. In the event that you don't consider their to be as isolated people yet as a wellspring of need satisfaction, it becomes conceivable sexual conduct.

However, in spite of the evident independence of people with NPD, they have serious relational needs. Their requirement for outer affirmation of their uncommonness implies they must be seeing someone that permit them to feel remarkable and respected. This overburdens their associations with their requests for confidence improving collaboration and is probably going to contribute pretty much nothing or nothing as a by-product of the delights they look for. E 'of focal significance in the NPD that favourable luck will come without anything consequently. E 'likely that people with NPD are attempting to address their own issues seeing someone without recognizing the free presence of those from whom "hope to be encouraged." If they are compelled to perceive the nearness of a supporter, disparage the blessing or the individual who gave it. Mates for people with NPD regularly have guardians with NPD who have influenced them to view misuse and dismissal as adoration.

People with NPD are inclined to contend with their companions, they need to be with somebody unique yet would prefer not to lose the spotlight. Inside connections, people with NPD expect appreciating respect, have an unequivocal love for themselves, and assume hypothetical responsibility for other people. Act with hatred toward those with whom they are included. They see their own accomplishments in gaudy and expanded while depreciating the commitments of others. Simultaneously, these people are very defenceless against analysis or being disregarded. At the point when their unrivalled position is in danger or when shown their absence of flawlessness, their self-idea may, for a period, plunge an analysis (or may have an upheaval of outrage). Without successful entrance of their resistances, nonetheless, people with NPD are satisfied with themselves and hope to be seen and recognized as extraordinary.

People who are experiencing NPD and are capable are regularly in places of power themselves. In the event that managing other power figures are not respectful, genial and deigning, and anticipate extraordinary treatment. Not uncover any data that may stigmatize them and act with vainglorious outrage when they are tested. Lying isn't troublesome, camouflage is a routine conduct. These people are reluctant to acknowledge that as far as possible additionally concern them.

Conduct in NPD is generally haughty. These people carry on in a self-important, vainglorious, pretentious, and scornful. They have no respect for his own trustworthiness and loaded with himself with detachment to the rights and needs of others. However, they can likewise show self-assuredness, social parity, security, potential for administration and results direction. Their aspiration and their self-assurance can prompt achievement, yet their presentation can be hindered by their bigotry of analysis. Their self-importance, people with NPD are strikingly sensitive.

They are effectively annoyed and feel abused. People with NPD additionally experience fatigue, disappointment and absence of satisfaction and significance in their work. It 'hard for these people to keep up long haul occupations where obligation regarding mistake or disappointment are progressively hard to cover up. People with NPD don't accept that equal social duties concern them. They anticipate that others should serve them without giving much consequently. They are hard, merciless and ailing in appreciation have hissy fits, verbal and psychological mistreatment, physical and sexual maltreatment since they accept that others ought to be basically worried to make them cheerful and make them agreeable. These people are especially ire and hatred for any individual who attempts to consider them responsible for their conduct exploitative and egotistical.

People with NPD are extensive and slanted to misrepresent, they centre on pictures and subjects and mistreat the realities. Utilize self-trickiness to protect their hallucination. They will effectively reinforce their prevalent status that is given without anyone else. They are serious, proud, restless, pompous, and extremely touchy. People with NPD proof a lopsided ethical quality and seem prepared to move esteems to accomplish their objectives, they can take part in neurotic lying.

The NPD influence is commonly impassive, imperturbable, and described by faked serenity. This progressions when people with NPD experience lost certainty. At that point they get furious and may encounter sentiments of disgrace and void. On the off chance that these people lose their narcissistic sentiments of simple prevalence, they become badly tempered, irritated, and subject to rehashed episodes of discouragement and embarrassment. People with NPD regularly experience outrage, ire and disappointed privilege. Disdain is the focal occasion of serious character issue and outrage that originates from the initial barely any long stretches of life, served to kill the torment however got valuable, later, to evacuate obstructions to satisfaction. People with NPD experience extreme jealousy, dread and outrage. They are especially furious when others don't accord them profound respect or regard. For these people, outrage is progressively average of disgrace and jealousy that is related with weakness, with a feeling of grotesqueness and barrenness.

People with NPD are caught in a sort of hair-splitting. They have ridiculous standards for themselves, at that point or persuade themselves that they have achieved these beliefs (the bombastic stance) or feel characteristically imperfect and fizzled (burdensome position). The NPD hallucination of prevalence is a feature of a summed up scorn for the real world. These people feel unconstrained by rules, customs, points of confinement and order. Their reality is made of self-fiction in which clashes are expelled, disappointments recovered, and pride in one's self is easily kept up. Effectively devise conceivable motivations to legitimize their conduct, egotistical and without thought for other people.

The recollections of past connections are regularly fanciful and evolving.

On the off chance that legitimizations and self-duplicity come up short, people with NPD are defenceless against disheartening, disgrace, and a feeling of vacancy. At that point they have little plan of action other than dream. They have a uninhibited and become mixed up in dreams of self-extolling. This is unmanageable through dream is curbed and kept out of mindfulness. As they reliably cheapen others, they don't scrutinize the rightness of what they accept; feel that the others are incorrect. The trademark challenges of people with NPD practically all come from their absence of strong contact with the real world. On the off chance that the bogus picture of self gets sufficient, their reasoning will get impossible to miss and freak. At that point their guarded moves become progressively straightforward to other people.

CHAPTER 12: SUBSTANCE DEPENDENCE IN NPD

Group B has the highest incidence of disorders co-occurring substance abuse among the three groups of personality disorders according to DSM-IV

Freud said that drugs can give pleasure and a greatly desired level of independence from the outside world, the drug allows the withdrawal from the pressures of reality. Individuals with NPD will always be attracted to drugs that support their inflated self-image and allow them to escape from a reality that they do not like. The independence from the outside world (and its insistent pressures based on reality) allows these individuals to remain unaware of their failures, waste, limitations and inability to self-regulate. The drug can become an alternative to live life their way.

However, their approach also requires constant attention and concern for the maintenance of abstinence and prevent relapse. Addiction becomes a disorder in its own right and should be treated directly. Nevertheless, therapy for personality disorders can lead to a profound change in the experience of self and the world by the individual suffering from disturbed personality, which, in turn, can positively affect recovery from addiction.

Individuals with NPD are vulnerable to abuse and addiction to drugs and alcohol:

- For the feelings of well-being domain and they offer;

- For the experience of wholeness and vitality;

- How wrong way and misunderstanding to matter and avoid a painful impact with reality;

- As part of a global model of narcissistic self-involvement and self-indulgence;

- For their need for a high level of stimulation;

- To give immediate relief from discomfort and a sense of self-importance and power;
-

- To calm tensions created by unrecognized hypersensitivity to evaluation.

The belief that we are unique and special is to separate these individuals from the recognition that they have developed a drug addiction. It also allows them to believe that they can escape the negative effects of addiction, and can easily stop using drugs. Maintain a grandiose belief, sometimes in extraordinary circumstances, to be able to manage their addiction. The grandeur of the NPD, which is crucial to maintaining the addiction, it is the presumption of a privileged exalted but impossible. The feelings are expressed great is exempt from the consequences of the behaviour that the laws of nature.

Individuals with NPD are vulnerable to abuse and addiction to drugs and alcohol because there are drugs that support an inflated sense of self and drugs that interrupt or moderate feelings of depression and low self-esteem. Most of these individuals use the drug that increases their feelings of vigour, power, or euphoria. Cocaine is very effective in achieving this goal. Individuals with NPD, to keep away the unwanted intrusion of unpleasant reality, they use denial, avoidance and hyper compensation supported by an increase in activity, hyper-productivity and grandeur. The use of these defences can result in an increase of the insulation. These individuals use alcohol and other sedatives to facilitate this isolation. There are some individuals with NPD who prefer autistic stimulation of hallucinogens.

Another factor in looking at the drug of choice of the NPD is the consummate skill required to handle the situation of drugs (including trade) and the centrality to others that the drug trade is encouraging. It 'possible that these activities may be more satisfying for individuals with NPD using the same drug.

CHAPTER 13: THERAPEUTIC TREATMENT IN NARCISSIST & NARCISSICM

The therapy of narcissistic disorder is very difficult, even for their total unawareness of the disorder and the effect that it causes in the other. Usually come to therapy only because they feel depressed, but the traditional antidepressant therapies are not effective. Cognitive therapy in the medium to long term (1 to 2 years) offers a chance for improvement, although it is very difficult to change a personality structure and, in these cases, even win the confidence of the patient and keep it high.

People who suffer from narcissistic personality disorder is difficult to perceive as "patients", even when access to specialists for a care pathway and the unconscious priority seems to be to get from the relationship with the other recognition and nourishment for one's self. L '"other" seems to be tolerated only "in use", not as a separate individual "for what it is." The relationship between physician and patient ranges from great distances and dangerous vicinity, including monologues which choke the other keeping it away and finding a neighbourhood almost fusion, through gruelling demands special attention and exclusive.

Individuals with personality disorders usually come to therapy with these problems in addition to those related to personality - most often with depression and anxiety. Often they see the difficulties they have with others as external and independent of their behaviour or input (Beck, 1990). Individuals with NPD do not tolerate the discomfort and very often come into therapy for depression. Depression in NPD is often carried by a crisis affecting the narcissistic grandiosity and reflects the discrepancy between expectations and fantasies of the NPD and reality.

Individuals with NPD may have trouble entering treatment because they live need help as demeaning and unacceptable. However, if you are in a crisis severe enough, they can also seek therapy to recover their feelings of confidence, a sense of superiority light and the ability to sustain themselves with the fantasy of self-glorification. Their view of themselves, their past, the current situation and what they need from therapy will be distorted by their need to be large. They'll resistance to a feed-back based on reality and can escape from the treatment setting if they are not sufficiently confirmed and comforted with an inflated view of themselves. You may need to cooperate with the narcissistic need support to develop a therapeutic relationship. However, a return to comfort for individuals with NPD may be all you are looking for and can leave the therapy in any case. Becomes a challenge for the evaluation and therapy communicate well enough with these individuals to allow realistic feedback and the development of more adaptive behaviours.

These individuals may also consider the drug as an indication of a personal flaw and does not intend to adapt. Overall, medications to individuals with NPD should first address the symptoms of any disorder co-occurring Axis I

Personality disorders are generally made for most crude and maladaptive traits that are privileged compared to more adaptive traits (even if there are adaptive traits within all personality disorders) Operators must be able to confirm individual subjects, suggesting an adaptive change and affirm adaptive behaviours without becoming openly responding to annoying quality that characterize the personality disorder in evidence.

Among the most important qualities for professionals who work with individuals with NPD are no defensiveness and competitiveness not authentic. Operators must find a way to feel comfortable with the idealization and the complaint critique of these subjects. Working with individuals with NPD sometimes involves the management of demands, expectations or unreasonable criticism. Their anger within the therapy is often the feeling of the subjects under which operators have failed to respond adequately to their needs confirmation, recognition and praise, over time it is virtually impossible to avoid disappointing these subjects. If the user responds negatively to self-magnification or the arrogance of NPD, even nonverbally, these individuals take criticism and experience living as a refusal.

For individuals with NPD, the validation of their thinking and their emotional experience is crucial to the growth of more adaptive skills. It seems that bring in therapy invulnerable armour of grandiosity, self-centralization, exhibitionism, arrogance and tendency to devalue others. Even the depression that lies beneath the arrogance is made of narcissistic rage and feelings of humiliation. Yet the psychological fragility is real and therapy for individuals with NPD must involve the problem of disappointment. Operators need to put in front of those with NPD aspects of reality that are denying, devaluing and avoiding. With firmness and tact, operators must discuss the grandeur, the sense of entitlement and arrogance of NPD remaining aware of the vulnerability that these subjects before the terrible shame in response to criticism they perceive. The process of therapy involves an annoying insistence by individuals with NPD in accusing others for their problems, assuming a position of superiority over the operators, and hearing constructive confrontation as a criticism humiliating. Yet, impatience, anger and counter-arrogance on the part of the operator are not productive and result in treatment failure.

The need for tact and caution has to do with the quality of the tenuous relationship with individuals with NPD. These individuals will flee any situation in which they feel that their self-esteem is diminished. They run away from their own mistakes and hide from people who might discover them. Individuals with NPD do not balance their self-approval with an ability to see and accept their own faults. Learn to tolerate his faults must be modelled by the operators through their clear of non-judgmental, accepting and realistic in relation to their shortcomings and human frailties. The comparison with individuals with NPD must be inserted in a strong support. However, it should also be clear, direct, repetitive and stationary to break the defenses put in place by people with NPD.

Traders may start to feel flattered and enjoy the company of people with NPD. Are beginning to feel a nuisance and a growing frustration at the fact that these individuals expect to get better when the operator actually does the work. The professional's aid may then start to feel devalued and work harder to get the approval of their subjects with NPD or become irritable, refuse and accuse.

Typical problems of countertransference with individuals with NPD are boredom, frustration and anger. Since these individuals are likely to ask for a lot and give very little, devalue others and be unable to respond to others with empathy, working with them is a very difficult process. Another counter transference disorder with these individuals is to feel forgotten and ignored as a real person. There is a sense, for operators, not to exist in the very room where the therapy takes place with the client NPD. Operators can be sleepy, irritable and unable to focus on the progress that you are working in therapy.

These individuals seem to give the impression that the purpose of the interview is only to approve its importance that promote themselves. However, they can be highly traumatic stories. Although individuals with NPD appear arrogant and powerful insight-oriented therapy may put them at risk of depression and suicidal tendencies because they experience the lies they say about themselves.

Cognitive therapy in the treatment of NPD draws on three basic components: grandiosity, hypersensitivity to criticism and empathy deficit. These individuals appear to have functional deficits about the self, the world and the future. Are considered special, exceptional and justified to focus on their own personal gratification at the expense of others. Expect admiration, respect and willingness on the part of others. Their expectations about the future have to do with the realization of grandiose fantasies. They do not believe that other people's feelings are important. Their behaviour is impaired by deficits in the ability to cooperate with others and to engage in mutual interaction. Implement behaviour too demanding and self-indulgent. Cognitive therapy conceptualizes NPD in terms of these dysfunctional beliefs and develops treatment to focus on these disorders.

The therapy interventions teach more adaptive methods of managing distress, improving interpersonal effectiveness, and building skills for affective regulation. Goals may not necessarily include personality logical restructuring. The focus of treatment should be adaptation, i.e., how these individuals respond to the environment.

If the apex of the development of personality is to develop the ability to take full responsibility for themselves - desires, behaviour and consequences of behaviour - a more adaptive functioning may in fact be a substantial success in therapy, and May, over time, lead to a more fundamental change in attitudes and behaviour.

If individuals with NPD should be ready to work in a better overall level of functionality, they can be ready to develop the quality of their adaptive personality style, rather than get stuck in a disturbed personality functioning. Personality style of the NPD is the self-confidence. These individuals without personality disorder have respect for themselves and believe in themselves and in their abilities, they are ambitious, they are able to take advantage of their strengths and their abilities, they can see themselves winning, they have balance and are masters of themselves, they know listen and accept criticism. Are outgoing, energetic, competitive. Are naturally suited to the policy and understand the structures of power. They can be leaders with and are able to work easily and effectively with others.

Working with individuals with personality disorders should not try to make them what they are not and what will never be. Since all personality disorders have forces and at least one positive potential, therapy should target the most adaptive expression of that particular personality style.

Treatment may include drug therapy, individual psychotherapy and psychotherapy group.

Drug therapy for the control of symptoms is often rejected by the patient, or followed with discontinuities, or abandoned to the first mild signs of improvement. The patient does not recognize the role of the psychiatrist and cannot trust, nor to trust: how then can propose adhesive and complacent, which are then translated into a consistent caring behaviour, aggressive mode and devaluing of open challenge; idealizing mode, which enhance the only doctor able to treat a case as exceptional, unlike the previous ones, all equally incompetent. Individual psychotherapy is affected by the same problems described above. Patients may present characteristics and lifestyles very different from each other, but they seem to share the lead in the room of idealization and devaluation intense psychotherapy, of himself as the therapist, making slow, problematic and uneven the establishment of a 'genuine alliance therapeutic.

Sometimes this alliance cannot be reached. The grandiose self of the patient may then occur either through contemptuous attitudes, both by applicants and companies: the therapist's behaviour is consistently interpreted "running" of person. In the experience of the patient, every gesture of the therapist may have a specific meaning attached to itself: for example, look for something more comfortable on your chair can be read by the patient as indifference to their story. These ways of relating to arouse in the therapist a wide range of feelings and experiences, ranging from anger, boredom and a refusal to attempt to present itself as a parental figure restorative.

The idealization can also offer a fast track, as ambivalent, to the satisfaction of narcissistic traits of the therapist. As for the parts not tolerable that the patient projects on him and the intense destructiveness, can sometimes be metabolized and sent back to the patient becoming important opportunities for greater recognition of the self and the therapist understood as "other," with needs, desires, gestures separate and independent.

The level of tolerance is subjective countertransference feelings and recognized by all professionals as staff and impassable limit to the continuation of the treatment.

A different time of treatment may include the adoption of combined techniques. Group psychotherapy seems to offer a good chance for patients with ongoing individual psychotherapy: group dynamics dilute negative transferences of the patient and the therapist's countertransference feelings. The advantages can be summarized in dealing with the difficulty to hold "a" place in the group (and not "all" the place), as well as in feedback relating to their destructiveness, also liable to contain.

In the field of psychoanalytical are highlighted, for their effectiveness, two main strategies. The first, proposed by Kornberg, is based on the test of reality, on the comparison and interpretation of the pathological grandiose self and negative transfer. The second, proposed by Kohut, is based on observations empathic and on the development of three modes of transfer (specular, idealizing / twin, alter-ego), in order to facilitate the correction of the structural deficits that characterize the narcissistic personality disorder.

There is also a third strategy, less used than before, which uses a method of investigation interpersonal active, alternating exploration empathy with the comparison of the transference-countertransference matrix. This strategy deals with the difficulties of individuals with narcissistic personality disorder to tolerate challenges to subjective perspectives and self-esteem; parallel to this, is characterized by the tendency to structure an active relationship with them oriented to the exploration of their interpersonal dynamics.

Family therapy and the torque are an important context within which individuals with narcissistic personality disorder have an opportunity, on the one hand, to become aware of the reactions that their way of being and behaving produces in others, the other to develop empathy and cooperative attitudes toward significant people, so then generalize the usual relations.

In both cases, it is noted that, generally, individuals with narcissistic personality disorder have access to treatment forming the reluctant member of the family or the couple and stating that "others are conducted to demonstrate the problems and to require changes, not them!"

The evidence in favour of a drug therapy for the treatment of narcissistic personality disorder are currently very poor, except for the cases in which use is made of it for the treatment of depressive symptoms or anxious, which most often motivates the request of therapy.

Meta-cognitive-interpersonal psychotherapy (TMI) for the treatment of narcissistic personality disorder aims primarily to reduce the suffering of individuals with this disorder, improving the quality of their lives.

A necessary condition for the achievement of this objective is the construction and regulation of the therapeutic alliance. This concept is the ability to create, between therapist and patient, a climate of mutual trust and respect, from the constant sharing of the various aspects of the therapeutic process (formulation of the problem, set goals, strategies pursued, techniques used, the tasks), in order to achieve a therapeutic use of the tools that is on the one hand as closely as possible to the specific patient, on the other hand able to support him in the understanding of the contents treated and the active participation in therapy.

Parallel to this, it is essential that the therapist is able to avoid harm to the therapeutic relationship, getting caught in the dynamics of interpersonal problems triggered by the narcissistic patient (detachment, competition, idealization-devaluation), rather than being able to use the relationship that is structure as a context favouring the awareness of dysfunctional aspects of its operation, so as to make possible corrective experiences on them.

From the above, the meta-cognitive-interpersonal treatment (TMI) is accomplished through the following steps:

- Identification of emotions, needs, desires, and access to them;
- Recognition of the relationship between internal states and relational variables;
- Identification, questioning and modification of core beliefs about themselves and others;
- Identification and interruption of the vicious circles that are established between thoughts, feelings and behaviour;
- Identification of problematic states (grandiosity, detachment, emptiness, depression, shame, envy, anger) and more functional evaluation of strategies for managing them;
- Reconstruction of dysfunctional interpersonal dynamics (detachment, competition, idealization devaluation) and passing them from the change in the

representation of self / other and expectations about the relationship;

- Open to the consideration of the feelings and perspectives of others.
- Regulation of self through the promotion of a more functional

The Dual diagnosis treatment must involve recognition of trends that encourage addictive behaviour, i.e., immaturity, escapism, and grandiosity. Must be taught new ways of dealing with feelings of powerlessness and helplessness other than compulsivity. Individuals with NPD feel rather uncomfortable seeing people as employees. In fact, these individuals tend to addictions hidden or secret for the contradiction that this behaviour has to want to project the image on the other. The fear of being discovered by fans can be a significant source of motivation for abstinence. However, their tendency toward denial, rationalization and imagination provide very strong support for the use of drugs and the denial of loss of control.

The dependence may be an attempt to cope with the fear without face directly. A feature of addiction can be avoidance - a tactic to escape. The cost of addiction varies only with the magnitude of compulsion, it is a form of servitude. The goal of therapy is to unravel a web of self-deception with regard to avoidance, escape and denial. For individuals with NPD the idea of servitude and the implications of the fear associated with escape behaviours can be quite unpleasant to enable them to consider abstinence as symbolic of their personal strength. The vision of themselves is to meet their psychological need to feel superior.

A dual diagnosis treatment to be successful for individuals with NPD must include: encouragement of appropriate dependency (people rather than drugs), the development of tolerance to feelings of sadness and despair, an increase in acceptance of the limits personal and emotional connection with others. Involvement in a group of the Twelve Steps can be quite positive for these individuals. AA in the sense of legitimacy is placed in comparison with humour and insight. Generous support is offered, but there is a subtle pressure to deal with the problem.

Individuals with NPD are particularly prone to relapse. They tend to be free from fear of relapse or believe that they can start a controlled use of what they have learned about addiction. Once you have fallen, individuals with NPD have problems important to return to therapy, in shame and humiliation. Part of the positive impact of relapse on therapy for these subjects is the acceptance of human limitations both as regards the power of the addictive process that as regards the need for help from others to remain abstinent.

Usually no need for a direct comparison to break the strong defenses of individuals with dual diagnosis of NPD. However, once the comparison becomes effective, the possibility of severe depression is significant and may require therapy. Abstinence may be a requirement for therapy and the use should lead to the end of the therapy. Both hypotheses emphasize the limits that apply to these individuals and their behaviour can have negative consequences.

CONCLUSION

Narcissists. They take you, chew you up, and spit you out, but once you get the dirt out of your eyes, everything becomes clearer. These individuals might not be the best to have around, and they can inflict serious damage on you and your mental wellbeing but helping yourself through recovery can uncover new layers of your person that you never knew existed.

While many are fortunate enough to live life without having to go through the abuse of a narcissist, those who do have a unique opportunity for learning. Not a lot of people are able to achieve the level of maturity that victims of narcissisticc abuse do, so you might say that you are fortunate in your own right.

Surviving narcissistic abuse is something you should be proud of. Not everyone can see it through, and not everyone has the resilience to defeat that kind of battle. But the simple fact that you're here and you're trying means that you do have what it takes to heal and recover from the pain.

Now, it's time to heal. It might have taken you a while, but you're here and you're on your way to a fuller, happier life, away from the abuse. So, take a deep breath, smile, and give yourself a pat on the back. It definitely wasn't easy.

CPSIA information can be obtained
at www.ICGtesting.com
Printed in the USA
BVHW010804260422
635265BV00017B/155